ST. ANDREWS

HOW TO PLAY
THE OLD COURSE
WITH TIP ANDERSON
AND DESMOND MUIRHEAD

ST.

ANDREWS

HOW TO PLAY THE OLD COURSE

BY DESMOND MUIRHEAD
AND TIP ANDERSON

WITH PHOTOGRAPHS BY BRIAN MORGAN

MAINSTREAM
PUBLISHING

Copyright USA 2000 by Desmond Muirhead and Tip Anderson
Photos copyright 2000 by Brian Morgan
All rights reserved

First published in Great Britain in 2000 by
MAINSTREAM PUBLISHING COMPANY (EDINBURGH) LTD
7 Albany Street
Edinburgh EH1 3UG

ISBN 1 84018 390 X

First published in the United States by
Newport Press
Suite 255, 1400 Quail Street
Newport Beach, CA 92660

A catalogue record for this book is available from the British Library

Designed and produced by Robert R. Reid
Printed in China by Toppan Printing Co. America Inc

CONTENTS

The fine Scottish town of St. Andrews provides a handsome background for the first and eighteenth holes of the Old Course. At right, the famous Swilcan Burn meanders across both fairways.

THE MANY FACES
OF ST. ANDREWS

I N THE ARCHIVE of the Royal and Ancient Golf Club of St. Andrews is a very old, well-thumbed leather-bound book. Across its frayed pages, inscribed in the large confident Victorian script taught to nineteenth-century British schoolboys, are thirty years' worth of suggestions to the R & A for the improvement of the links at St. Andrews. Improvements, did you say? Are you referring to the Old Course? What nerve!

Listening to some remarks about the Old Course, you might think the Almighty himself had shaped a golf course from the barren, sandy surface of the Links. "The Old Course has no parallel anywhere because its fashioning owes more to nature than to the hand of man," runs a typical assertion. Alister Mackenzie, who designed great golf courses on four continents, was certain no calculating hand had ever touched the Old Course. "In the early days of St. Andrews," Mackenzie wrote, "no one knew anything about golf course architecture. It may even have been planned by someone who had never seen a golf course."

Although that may be true of its earliest days, our memories could stand a little jogging concerning St. Andrews. It's only in the last few decades, forgetting its rather obscure past, that we've insisted on looking at the Old Course as unchangeable. Listen to Old Tom Morris – who officially cared for it until 1903 – talk about the dramatic changes he had seen in the Old Course over his long life. "If ever you should write anything about St. Andrews Links," he once told a member famous more for writing about golf than playing it, "begin with the High Hole, for it has given me more bother than all the rest of them put together."

The hole itself was rarely moved in the old days, unlike the modern practice of cutting fresh cups each day. "The hole was a great deal nearer the Eden in our young day than it is now," said Old Tom, reminiscing at the turn of the twentieth century, "and the neighborhood of the hole was ever changing because the hole itself sometimes filled up after a heavy storm at sea. The water drifted up with the gale, and the putting green was often little better than a bunker." The solution, said Old Tom, was to plant Dutch sea-lyme grass on the Eden banks to fix the soil. "A new green has been made at a lower level on the ground reclaimed by the lyme grass."

How could men familiar with this tale believe the Old Course was ever fixed and permanent? Ecological change alone, the wind and weather that formed the links, denies a static landscape. Alister Mackenzie himself summarized some of the Old Course's structural changes. "This much is certain," he wrote in the early 1930s, "that previous to 1859, the inward nine holes – with the exception of the eighteenth – were originally played back of the holes doing duty for the outward nine. As more golfers gave rise to congestion, fresh holes were cut for the inward half."

The Links has always been a working landscape. The debate over sheep grazing on the Old Course continued well after World War I; the sheep often damaged the greens, and the rabbits were another story altogether. The Laird of Strathtyrum, master of the estate that once controlled the links, still has the right to harvest shell rock from the links. He graciously exercises it only on the Eden Course, not the Old, and paves the roads on his farm with the proceeds.

The members of the R&A whose ideas fill the old suggestion book well knew the course was changing, and always had done. They understood that the bunkers added early in the twentieth century were a defense against the greatly increased distances players could realize with the rubber-cored ball. Had it not been for the gutta percha, that cheap industrial substitute for the labor-intensive and very expensive featherie, the gentlemen of the R&A might have carried on with their modest hobby in relative obscurity.

In an ironic consequence of golf's popularity – the revenge of the featheries, perhaps – the R&A also promoted a steady destruction of the whins, which effectively widened the fairways. At the earliest British Opens played at St. Andrews, the galleries were small, but by 1900 crowds of keen spectators would

Tip and Arnold Palmer discussing the next shot.

Tip and Desmond during their walk around the Old Course.

follow the competitors. For this reason, the whins were steadily reduced. That, as much as the length of drives with the new rubber-cored ball, pulled some of the sharp teeth from the Old Course. Consequently, the R&A created more than two hundred new bunkers before the 1905 Open. Horace Hutchinson, an influential member, wrote in 1905 that these bunkers were essential to save the challenging nature of the Old Course, "because the course had grown so much wider than it used to be, because of the virtual destruction of the whins."

It is still true today for the good players that there is little original trouble remaining from the whins on the Old Course, for the gorse is on the edges of play, and rarely catches shots. Indeed, the New Course asserts itself more strongly in this feature, thus preserving one of St. Andrews's revered traditions. The *old* Old Course – the one known to a *young* Old Tom Morris, if that locution can be forgiven – had a line of play out and back along the narrow spine of the Old Course's "singular" fairways. There was only this single route out and back, a think corridor of play. The course was shaped like a long waist that flared out at the hip of the greens, which grew even more pronounced when the famous double greens were created around 1830, according to the best guess of the R&A historian. In Old Tom Morris's youth, the efforts of Sir Hugh Lyon Playfair, Provost of the City of St. Andrews and an avid golfer, did much to resurrect the links. Old Tom recalled that before Playfair's time, the links "were very little more than an untrodden waste." This is not to denigrate nature so much as to praise what man has done. Golf is an invention, not, as some would have it, a divine gift, and while we may celebrate the pleasure it brings us, it's best to remember that we are singing of ourselves when we do so.

With the many *fin de siècle* alterations, another modern note was sounded. By July of 1905, according to an angry complaint in the Suggestion Book, a round of golf took "almost three hours – and there was a long wait on every tee!" One can sense the outrage dripping from the offended member's pen. For all of that, the Old Course is rightly revered as the great shrine of golf, the lure for tens of thousands of pilgrims annually. As a practicing golf course architect, I, too, have looked to the Old Course for inspiration, admired its subtlety, learned from its features. Dear old Alister Mackenzie based at least six of Augusta National's holes on the Old Course, and I myself have designed a Japanese course called New St. Andrews, which borrows ideas embodied in these ancient links. I find there is always something new to learn from the Old Course; it really does reward a lifetime's study.

No one, arguably, knows the Old Course as does Tip Anderson, famous in the Kingdom of Fife as the St. Andrews Boys Champion long before he gave a boost to an upstart American's career by guiding him around the Old Course during the Centennial Open Championships of 1960, and beyond. For thirty years, Tip Anderson marched alongside his friend Arnold Palmer. Bobby Jones, who also revered the Old Course beyond all others, achieved his quadrilateral Grand Slam, but Tip Anderson earned the caddie's trilateral by carrying for three British Open Champions in four years – Palmer twice, and Tony Lema once. But it's Palmer's name that is linked to Tip's, and Tip's to the Old Course. I can still see Tip's lean frame outlined against the clear sky above the North Sea as he huddles with Palmer and hands him a club. "That'll be a five iron, sir," I can hear him say, as he backs away.

You have to play the Old Course many times before you know its range of detail. You have so many choices on each shot, and hazards of so many different sizes and degrees of difficulty. The Old Course seems to have a basic intelligence woven into it, with an almost infinite range of strategic and analytic possibilities.

For my own pleasure and for research for this book, I made several trips to St. Andrews in 1991 to study the Old Course, both alone and in the company of Tip Anderson. Brian Morgan, the great Glaswegian photographer who like me is a member of the St. Andrews Club – whose fine clubhouse is hard by the eighteenth green – spent months finding the perfect light to photograph the Old Course in each of its restless, complicated, provocative moods.

Please join us as Tip and I wander about the Old Course, divining its contours and stratagems, its ambushes and disguises, its mysterious interludes and stark certainties.

– DESMOND MUIRHEAD

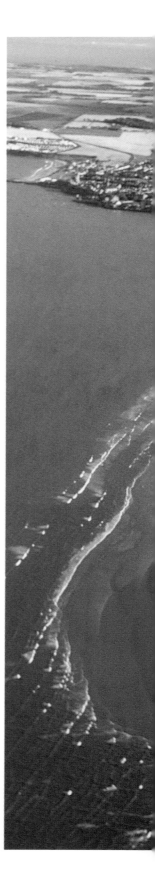

*The four courses at St. Andrews: left to right, the
Jubilee, the New, the Old, and the Eden.*

THE SWILCAN BURN

1

370 YARDS · PAR 4

*An aerial view of the first hole (on the left), showing the
Swilcan Burn winding across the first and eighteenth
fairways, sometimes spelling disaster for unwary golfers.*

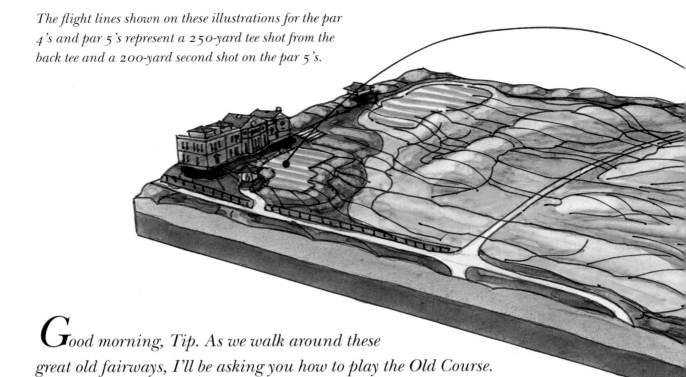

Good morning, Tip. As we walk around these great old fairways, I'll be asking you how to play the Old Course.

Good morning, Desmond. It's a beautiful day for golf; the sun is shining, the wind is light. Some would say that's unusual for St. Andrews.

D: Here we are at the first, which has been called the widest fairway in Christendom.

T: The first hole is playing into the west wind today. It is going to play long, but I always think that the course plays easier when the wind is from the west. That's because the last six holes – which come back to the R&A Clubhouse and play west to east – are much easier with this westerly wind behind the player, whereas – excluding the last hole – when those last five holes are *into* the east wind, they are the five most difficult holes you would ever want to play. Today, playing into wind, the pro could hit his driver; but on the day when there's nae wind or with a helping wind, he would probably hit a two iron.

D: This is a good first hole, the gateway to the course. The first hole of a golf course is your introduction to the architect, or in this case architects, God and man. The wide, flat fairway is inviting. There are usually many people watching. Behind us, this grand old pile, the Royal and Ancient Clubhouse, is imposing and slightly sinister. Way down in front of the green is a dark shadow, the Swilcan Burn, and that also is slightly sinister. From the tee, you can see the town, the golf course, the beach, and the sea, and some of the mood of the rest of the course comes through. What would you look for, Tip, on this hole if you were playing it for the first time?

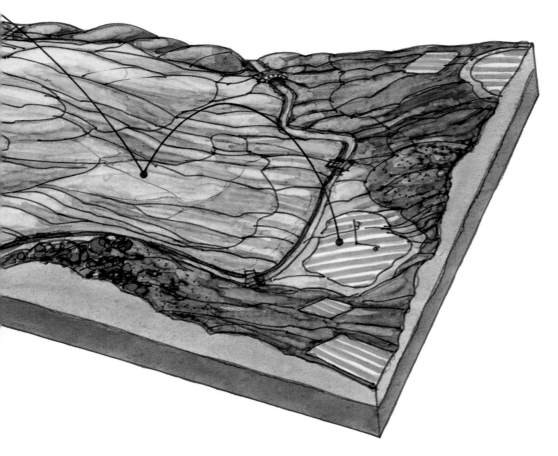

T: Ye must keep the ball out of the Burn and in play, that's the thing. I'm amazed how many good golfers end up in the Burn and how many high handicappers go out of bounds over that fence on the right, especially when they have this huge double fairway to aim at.

D: Normally, I don't like a tough hazard like the Burn on the opening hole, before the golfer has time to warm up. But with this wide fairway, which has no bunkers, and the large green, you need something to give the hole bite. Here you have a theme – placid fairway, strong hazard. This contrast of war and peace seems to haunt the Old Course. How would you play this hole, Tip, if you were a low handicapper?

T: In a tournament, ye want to play it as close to the bridge as possible to get a wide angle to the green and direct the ball into the slope. There are nae bunkers on the green, either, just the Burn, but that can be bad enough since it's right up against the putting surface. If ye play to the left, ye're also playing away from the out of bounds.

D: The first green is four or five times as big as a green on the average golf course. On a green of this size, you'd want to know where the hole was cut.

T: Aye, if the hole is cut in the middle of the green, for most players it's a straightforward nine iron, or thereabouts. On the first day of the Open, they'll cut the hole closer to the Burn. If it's within twelve or fifteen feet of the edge, ye'll need as much angle as ye can get.

D: Most of the players are serious golfers here, but not all of them can work the ball. How about the less-skilled golfer? What advice do you have for him?

Looking down the first fairway from the tee. With out-of-bounds on the right, the wise golfer hits well left on this wide, bunkerless fairway.

*The Starter's Hut
at the first tee.*

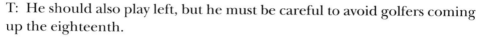

T: He should also play left, but he must be careful to avoid golfers coming up the eighteenth.

D: That may be the reason he so often hits it out of bounds. How does the average golfer play his second or third shot to the green?

T: He should aim for the middle, as both the back and front of the green have problems. If the second shot goes over the green, it's into deep rough. If ye hit to the back of the green, ye have rolls and a very difficult downhill putt. Obviously, ye want to steer clear of the Burn.

D: (*Observing the green*) At the front of this green is the Burn. Severe rolls both at the back and to the left would leave you quite a bit of work. So you're better off going for the center, unless you have very good control. This hole looks very easy, but many golfers are grateful for a four here.

T: Aye, especially if there's a wind. Some even play short of the Burn and chip on from there. With the prevailing wind behind, ye must make sure ye take enough club to clear the Burn easily. If that leaves ye with a long putt back, ye must watch the wind or your putt will go into the Burn. In a following wind, ye will almost always have a long putt, but it will be easier to control as the putt itself is now into wind.

D: With a green that big, you'd think it would be hard to miss, yet I know that Palmer, Trevino, and Nicklaus have all been in the Burn in tournaments. I understand Trevino said it was not a Burn, but a lousy creek.

T: He called it a lot worse than that.

D: Could you explain, Tip, why so many good golfers get in the Burn?

The first green runs tight up against the Burn, so the best angle to chip up to the pin is from the left side of the fairway.

T: Yes, I can give you an example. Sometimes in St. Andrews, the westerly wind can blow very strong. In the Open Championship of 1970, I remember Tom Shaw hit a three wood here for his *second* shot. He'd won a couple of tournaments the year before on the U.S. Tour, so he was playing well. That second shot, though, ran to the back of the green. Then he putted back into the Burn! The ball just did na' stop. That's your wind and your steep slope for you. He went back across the bridge, took a penalty drop, and chipped back over the Burn into the hole for a five! That's a hell of a five. Hard to believe that a professional golfer of that caliber would have to hit a three wood for his second shot there, but that's how it can blow. On a more normal day, it's a nine iron or a pitching wedge. I once caddied for a fellow I'd never seen before and when he hit a good drive down to a place where I'd normally give him a six iron, I handed him a five wood. He was still twenty yards short of the Burn after he hit. I could na' believe it. But we came to terms after a couple of holes. Caddies pride themselves on being able to size up a golfer rapidly. They can estimate how far a player would normally hit each iron as soon as he's hit a few shots. Then, they simply club him accordingly. They don't tell him the yardage, they just hand him a club. Sometimes they will give false yardage to persuade the player to use enough club. I was very embarrassed when my player came up twenty yards short, because as he hit it, I said: "That's a hell of a golf shot." I was as surprised as anyone. The wind got it, and it almost came right back to us like a boomerang. The wind was blowing fifty or sixty miles an hour.

D: When you get up close, the Burn is cut square like a bathtub and has a static feel. The water just lays there very still. It's a good hazard, you are either in the Burn or not. There's no halfway. The sides of the Burn are lined with stone and railroad ties. These materials have both found their way to American golf courses.

T: Most golf courses in Scotland are close to a railroad line, and ties were cheap.

D: Yes, and Scotland has exported many stone masons to other countries.

T: There's more wood than stone on Scottish courses, though. Stone is rare. It's too expensive.

D: As you grow familiar with the course, you get used to the square cut of the Burn. The form is honest, like the rest of the course; this course has those rare ingredients – integrity of design and maintenance.

T: You get what you see on the Old Course.

D: I notice the Burn's cut five feet wide across the green, and up to twelve feet wide along the fairway. We know the average golfer controls his distance better than his direction, so the Swilcan Burn is a harder hazard for him than for the professional. At the moment, the water in the Burn is three or four feet deep, yet often there's no water at all. The Burn must be tidal?

T: Yes, the tide flows into it and backs up; when there's nae water, you can play out of it. Sometimes the greenkeeper will catch the fresh water in it for use in irrigation. However, it's never easy to play from the Burn.

D: I understand that before they built the bulkheads, clumps of grass grew along the banks and they had trouble with flooding the fairway.

T: Years ago, the rough was a lot longer on this course.

D: Now that the edges are cleaned up, the Burn is sort of formal, less natural-looking, but a much more reasonable golf hazard, I think. I noticed in a photo taken of the gallery during the 1927 Open Championship that crowds of excited people – even women in tight skirts – were jumping over the Burn near the stone bridge. The great Bobby Jones was winning his second consecutive Open that year, and no doubt they were running to watch him.

T: Aye, he was very popular in this city, just as Palmer is today with both women and men. Almost every great player has either won or been very close in the Open Championship on this course. Look at the last four winners: Nicklaus twice, Ballesteros, Faldo, and now Daly.

D: They tell us that St. Andrews is over five hundred years old. That's back in the Middle Ages! But, golf courses change over the years. We know a lot about the greens and bunkers on the Old Course, but would you say that the turf is still the same as when you were a boy?

T: There is more grass today on the Old Course than there ever was. Walter Woods, the superintendent who is in charge of all six courses at St. Andrews, has improved this course beyond recognition. Twenty or thirty years ago, it looked more like a desert than a golf course. Even in 1995, it was pretty brown just before the Open.

D: There are a lot of daisies this year. They're attractive, but bad for golf. How long do they last?

T: We canna' let them last. He has na' yet this year, but Walter will use a herbicide to kill them. There's na' been enough rain or warmth to get strong turf growth. At the moment, if we took the weeds out, the course would look pretty bare.

D: Do you think the green on this hole has changed as well as the fairway?

T: Aye, I do. Nowadays, the fellows can fly it straight to the stick even when the hole is quite close to the Burn, whereas in the old days, they had to bounce it over the Burn to get close because the ground was so hard. Irrigation has made the course much easier.

D: Besides the gorse, or whins, as you call them, which we can see to the right of the Burn on this first hole, there's a wide variety of foreign plants in both green and fairway on the Old Course.

T: That's always been true. This is a real linksland, reclaimed from the sea. The grasses have always been here, they are natural to St. Andrews.

THE GRASSES

THE GRASS GROWS a lot slower here than further south, or in America. There are also many different grasses in the greens. First, there are the bents; then the fine-leafed fescues, which are the mainstays of the Old Course greens. The chartreuse-colored weed grass, *Poa annua*, is even encouraged here because it grows well in damp weather and fills in the bare patches. Finally, there is perennial rye, and sometimes a few common weeds like daisies.

These greens on the Old Course cannot be treated like greens in America where the summers are much warmer than in Scotland. In this cool climate, the greens are quite vulnerable and are getting too much wear, so they're dependent on warm weather to promote more growth.

Many links courses are exposed to less than ten thousand rounds a year, but this course endures forty-five thousand. And that number is really more like ninety thousand because almost every group has ten people in it – four players, their caddies, plus a couple of admiring friends or spouses tagging along to record their visit for posterity. Besides the golfers' feet, winds and birds scatter seed among the gorse and wild grasses, and both have left their mark all over the Old Course. Residual weeds are sometimes good indicators of soil quality – brambles and nettles, for example, usually grow in good soil, while ground elder, horsetails, and heather (*Calluna vulgaris*) are thriftiest in poor soil. There is also a host of circumglobular coast erosion weeds growing on the Old Course – borages, dogtails, ragworts, clovers, chickweeds, yarrows, cocksfoot, and plantains, which, with their broad, flat leaves, are a real nuisance.

THE DYKE

411 YARDS · PAR 4

The second hole, on the right, shares with the sixteenth hole one of the huge double greens for which the Old Course is famous. There are severe undulations as these greens were originally found and mowed in situ.

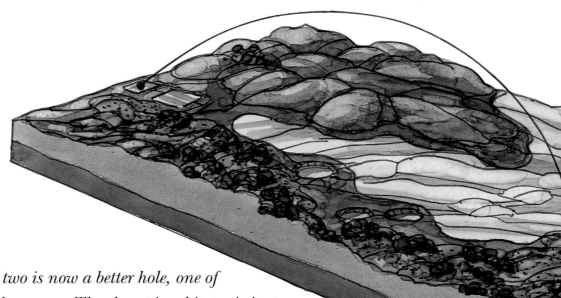

T: Number two is now a better hole, one of the best on the course. The championship tee is just at the middle tee. Today, a professional golfer would hit a driver aimed on the left corner of the trees in the distance. If there was no wind, he would have to hit a one or two iron because of Cheape's Bunker. It's two hundred forty yards away, and a nasty one, too. But today, we can use a driver, and we must keep it to the right. We will still have only a six or seven iron into the green from the ideal spot in the fairway, which is twenty yards in front of Cheape's.

D: The course narrows quite a bit here on these two parallel holes, numbers two and seventeen, and the whins are heavy. They must scare quite a few golfers.

T: Oh yes, an amateur once hit it over the drying sheds on number seventeen from the second tee. That's a hundred fifty yards off line. This hole is more typical of St. Andrews than number one, although three holes on the Old Course are flat and open like number one. There's the eighteenth, of course, and then nine and ten.

D: Don't you think that twelve and fifteen would also qualify?

T: I suppose they would.

D: These six open holes appear so benign they give an interesting balance to the course and provide a sharp contrast with the other holes.

T: If you are a good enough player, ye should never go left on this hole, especially na' in tournaments. If the pin's on the left, it's much better to be on the right of the fairway. It's true there are dangerous bunkers there, but the touring pro or good amateur would rarely find them. The hole opens out past the first group of whins, so if ye can hold your line to the left, or even to the center of the trees, ye're in good shape. Can ye see the cottage in the trees? The pin for tournaments is often in line with that cottage, and there's a bunker right before the flag.

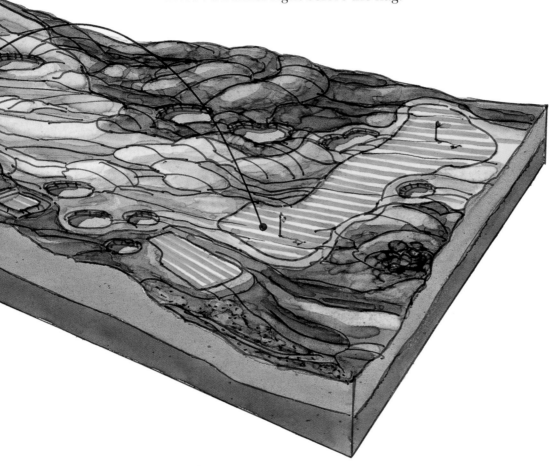

D: (*Standing in the middle of the fairway and looking back*) This is the block of whins that you have to hit over. They don't look as bad from here, so probably the average player could enjoy this hole. How far away from the tee are we at this point?

T: About a hundred twenty yards. For safety, ye'd have to carry at least that far, but that's not much unless ye're into a strong wind.

D: In spite of its tough appearance from the tee, the drive is a very reasonable one to the landing area, which is relatively level. On this fairway, you have rough and gorse and rolls, then a smoother passage after almost two hundred and fifty yards.

T: (*Walking toward the green*) See this place here? In tournaments, they put the pin behind the bunker. If ye're on the left or on the seventeenth fairway, ye don't have much of a shot into the green. But if ye're on the right-hand side, ye have a much better shot in; ye can really see where ye're going. For a championship, the pins are never down there where we see them today. That area is used for normal, everyday play. During the championship, the cottage down the way is still the best line for the pin.

D: You are saying, Tip, that the more daring you are and the more you go to the right, the more you are rewarded with an easier second shot. I take it that the more timid you are, the more you will play to the left to   avoid the whins, and then you are penalized with an increasingly difficult second. That's the classic ratio of risk to reward – another of the founding principles of golf course architecture.

T: Most of the holes on this course follow that principle, but there's always quite a bit of luck involved in links golf. If the pin is up here (*Pointing to the upper part of the green*), it's almost a blind second shot.

D: Even if you walk over to the right of the pin, you can hardly see the bottom of the flagstick. You really have to hit an accurate second, but even then you can't see where your ball lands.

T: No, ye never see the bottom of the flagstick at all.

D: That large, serpentine mound in front bars it from view. What's the point of having all this green on the right, then?

T: All the greens have been enlarged lately to accommodate increased play.

The second tee: aim for the middle of the stand of trees in the distance. Just remember that Cheape's Bunker is 240 yards out on the left.

D: Perhaps the flat area looks larger than it actually is, as this part of the green merges with the flatness of the third tee. The second green really has its own Valley of Sin, like the depression in front of the eighteenth green. This is a larger green than that one, but nothing like as big as the fifth. My friend Henry Longhurst (known affectionately as Henry Longthirst for his liking of drink) used to say the Hole O'Cross covered two and a half acres – which is about a hundred thousand square feet. Yet, today it's only one and a half acres, or about sixty thousand square feet in area. (As a parenthetical note for history buffs, this green looks bigger in Alister Mackenzie's plan of 1924, but the tees are included in the map of the green.)

T: Henry said that, did he? Now that the winter green has been enlarged, it's hard to believe that Hole O'Cross was ever any bigger. It's enormous, anyway.

D: It's not true, is it, that Alexander the Great camped his entire army on that green, or was it in Cockle Bunker?

T: I don't think he came this far north.

D: Even with the sun, this wind today is really cold. One feels lucky to hang on to one's ears, nose, and fingers. I'm glad I'm wearing this thick sweater. Caddieing in winter must be very cold.

T: They say we Scots are used to the cold, but that's the reason why I don't caddie much in winter. As for that blind pin position, the pin is always up to the left in a championship. The shot always catches much more wind when it's put on the top plateau of the green, and this makes for difficult putting.

Always carry onto the green. Runup shots shot here can bounce to either side.

The pin position during a championship is often about eight yards above the bunker in the front of the green.

D: That's a tough placement for any golfer. That front bunker would turn you to stone; it must be at least eight feet deep, but looks as bottomless as Loch Ness. The turf wall is vertical, and then there's the mound on the right side, which is covered with rough. Pity the poor fellow whose ball gets stuck in there. Surely, you'll need three putts to get down from the bottom level of the green; the ridge on the left really drops down from the upper plateau to this lower level.

T: It's three-putt range, all right. If ye get down in two, it's a bonus.

D: (*Looking at the flat area in front of the green, which is next to the bunker*) If you hit on that piece of hard ground, the ball will bounce onto the green – the famous St. Andrews run up – but you'd have to be fortunate with the bounce. Would you say it's better percentage golf if you play the ball all the way onto the green?

T: Always carry it onto the green. Some holes require a run up, although if you bounce it in front of this number two green, the ball won't carry true but will bounce to one side or the other. Of course, ye must be careful not to overclub or ye'll go into the Wig bunker at the back. That's a difficult one.

D: Where would the flag for this adjoining sixteenth green be placed during the championship?

T: Just on top of the first hill. There's a sort of ridge across the green, and the flag is placed along that ridge during championships. If the flags are at all close on the double-greens, they wait for oncoming golfers to hole out. The man on the back nine has the right of way.

D: The present flag for number sixteen is pretty close to the flag on this number two hole, which must be confusing sometimes. When there is no one to control things, you've got a frightening piece of green over the front of number two, with a very difficult putt up from it.

T: That's another recent extension from Walter Woods. He's made another sixty square yards or so of green. The pin is always up top during a championship. The lower greens are called winter greens. They're mostly used in winter, and for nontournament play. It's an easier hole from the lower part of the green.

D: They rest the upper green in winter, but that doesn't change the approach shot, does it? This number two at the front really is the strangest looking green. These rolls remind me of buffaloes just beneath the surface, galloping across the green, humped backs and all. Those are twelve to fifteen percent grades on the slopes, with up to three-foot humps on those front rolls, and all within a few feet. If I designed a green like that in America, they'd plant me with the buffaloes, only deeper.

T: Those are pretty severe rolls, but Walter has just extended the green over the existing ground, and mowed it. This is the traditional way of making greens on links courses.

D: I can see a set of four small bunkers surrounding the medal tee for the third hole. They don't seem to be doing much.

T: Aye. They're well out from the green, though, so not in play for a championship.

THE WHINS

THE GORSE, OR WHINS (*Ulex europea*), are dense, prickly leafed native shrubs, covered with glorious yellow flowers in May. In the springtime, these broad masses of deep color turn the Old Course into a radiant flower show, which finds a color-coded complement in the pale blue sky. The whins are also one of the most deadly hazards ever found on a golf course. If you get in them, it very often means a lost ball, but if you thresh around enough, you might find someone else's ball, left there from a previous round. Or, you may not find anything at all. You have to remember this is Scotland, and lost balls are a local industry. Even if you find your ball, it is almost impossible to play out of the whins without damaging your back. Years ago, the whins were much more extensive on the Old Course, but play was getting slower and slower so various committees had the whins cut back, and they were cleared completely from certain areas. This was done in the late 1800s and early 1900s. Since then, they've been cut back further to make more room for spectators. More recently, they've been artfully incorporated into the design of the different holes by Walter Woods, his committees, and maintenance crews. Whins spread by growth and seed, but are now carefully managed. Because of their random growth, large groups of whins have a sprightly, spontaneous look that contributes to the erroneous idea that St. Andrews is a completely natural golf course, untouched by the hand of man. The number of whins, however, seems to me to have increased in the last ten years.

CARTGATE OUT

352 YARDS · PAR 4

*Cartgate Bunker is a huge cavern with the
green on the right.*

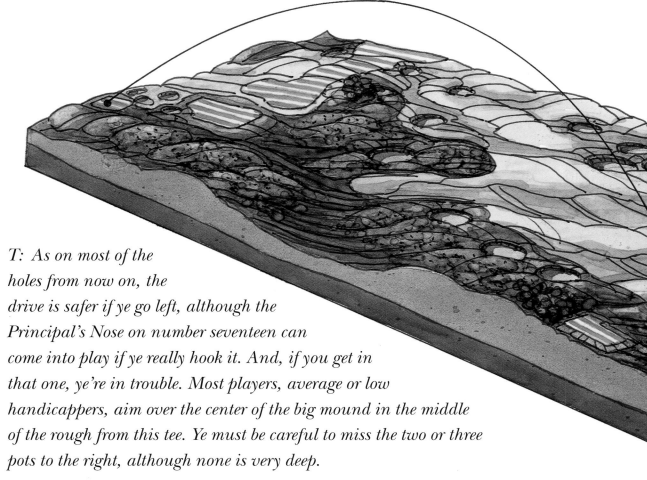

T: As on most of the holes from now on, the drive is safer if ye go left, although the Principal's Nose on number seventeen can come into play if ye really hook it. And, if you get in that one, ye're in trouble. Most players, average or low handicappers, aim over the center of the big mound in the middle of the rough from this tee. Ye must be careful to miss the two or three pots to the right, although none is very deep.

D: For some reason, I find this hole one of the least memorable on the Old Course, although it's typical enough of St. Andrews. The tee shot is blind, and it looks ferocious with all this hummocky, rolling rough and whins to shoot over, but the carry is short – especially from the front tees, which give the average golfer a chance. When you get to the green, you'll meet the Cartgate Bunker – semicircular, with a clean vertical face of turf bricks. It's very deep and long. The front of the bunker parallels the fairway, so a shot to the right must miss it entirely, but that opens up the green. Conversely, a shot to the left must carry more of the bunker.

T: Aye, if ye play left, ye can't see the green so well. Then it's a much harder shot to hold the green.

D: Frankly, I like these higher tees. They're better when you've got this heavy stuff in front of you. How often do they use them?

T: Never in a championship. None of us like them. They're only about ten years old. The lower and medal tees are the only ones used for champi-

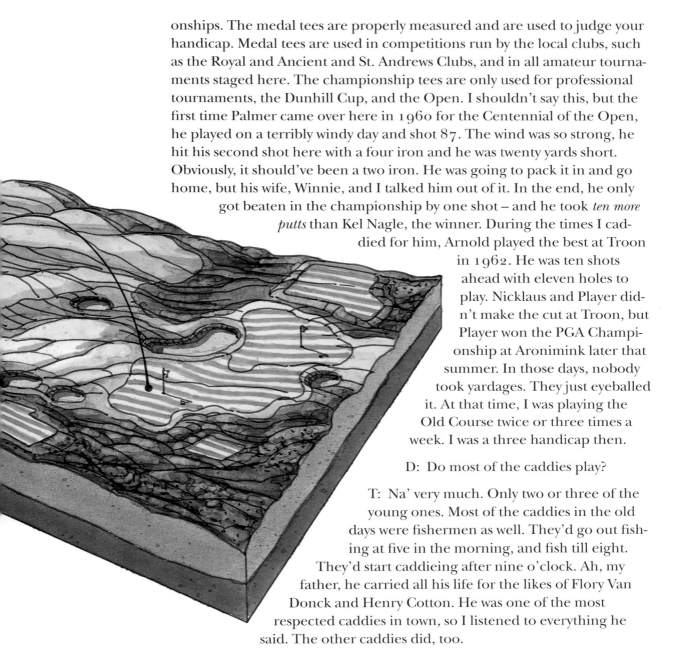

onships. The medal tees are properly measured and are used to judge your handicap. Medal tees are used in competitions run by the local clubs, such as the Royal and Ancient and St. Andrews Clubs, and in all amateur tournaments staged here. The championship tees are only used for professional tournaments, the Dunhill Cup, and the Open. I shouldn't say this, but the first time Palmer came over here in 1960 for the Centennial of the Open, he played on a terribly windy day and shot 87. The wind was so strong, he hit his second shot here with a four iron and he was twenty yards short. Obviously, it should've been a two iron. He was going to pack it in and go home, but his wife, Winnie, and I talked him out of it. In the end, he only got beaten in the championship by one shot – and he took *ten more putts* than Kel Nagle, the winner. During the times I caddied for him, Arnold played the best at Troon in 1962. He was ten shots ahead with eleven holes to play. Nicklaus and Player didn't make the cut at Troon, but Player won the PGA Championship at Aronimink later that summer. In those days, nobody took yardages. They just eyeballed it. At that time, I was playing the Old Course twice or three times a week. I was a three handicap then.

D: Do most of the caddies play?

T: Na' very much. Only two or three of the young ones. Most of the caddies in the old days were fishermen as well. They'd go out fishing at five in the morning, and fish till eight. They'd start caddieing after nine o'clock. Ah, my father, he carried all his life for the likes of Flory Van Donck and Henry Cotton. He was one of the most respected caddies in town, so I listened to everything he said. The other caddies did, too.

D: You inherited quite a bit of knowledge.

T: That's true. I picked up everything quickly, even golf. I only played for eighteen months before I became St. Andrews Boys Champion. But these young caddies – I try to tell them something, but they say "No, no," and won't listen, so I've stopped trying to tell them anything. I was lucky enough to win eighteen trophies, among them the one mentioned and the following year, the Fife Boys Championship. That's the county championship. Then, I had to do my national service – Royal Artillery from 1950 to l952. Luckily, I wasn't sent overseas. I won two army tournaments. One of them was at Royal Birkdale, which helped me a lot when I caddied for Arnold in the 1961 Open Championship there, which we won. Otherwise, I did na' do much work in the army. I was always playing football or golf. I was in the quartermaster's stores, one of the cushiest jobs in the army.

D: When you get to the landing area, the carry looks worse. You have about a hundred eighty yards on the drive over this really hairy ground and whins. You have to clear a huge, shaggy mound with the six-foot-deep walled bunker known as Cheapes, which rises almost one hundred thirty yards off the tee. I guess you aim over the center of the mound, is that right? What an intimidating visual hazard that is for the average player, and what a frightening shot into the wind.

A ferocious-looking panorama greets golfers at this tee, but all golfers can carry it from any of the tees.

T: Aye, but watch out for the pots to the right. They can be bad. If ye hit too far right, you're on the New Course, but fortunately ye're allowed to play off that. Most of the holes on the Old Course are not extra long, but they are wide open to the wind, especially on these large greens, and there's no shelter to be found. So, when allowing for borrow on the greens, ye'll be thinking more of the wind than the slope.

D: In America, *borrow* and *break* are identical terms. The landing area for this hole is none too hospitable, and you'll be lucky to get a level lie. As you draw nearer the green, the whins seem rather pathetic as they thin out toward the open areas. They're quite gaunt, actually, and you can see beneath them where low grasses struggle to emerge. There's hardly any true fairway on this hole; it all looks like trampled rough, and then you have these giant mounds leering at you as you approach the green.

T: Number three is a short hole if there's nae headwind. The green has a left-to-right slope.

D: There are some heavy rolls behind the present pin position and more big rolls on the left, with a monster bunker elbowing into the center front of the green. For all that, I would say the green is the most attractive and forgiving of the first three. To me, number three is a beautiful green, safely undulating. Some greens just seem to feel friendly, don't they?

T: Don't underestimate this green. On the putts, remember, ye must allow for wind *and* slope, but if ye're away from the big rolls, the greens on this course are generally very flat and even. The rule is, For anything less than fifteen feet, unless ye can see an absolute, definite borrow that is really obvious, it's a straight putt.

D: This is another risk-versus-reward hole.

T: Yes, the more ye go left, the safer the drive but the harder the second shot. Ye'll want to bounce it so that the ball will run into the green – a flat, running shot if the pin is at the front.

D: Whereas, if you bounce the ball on that ridge dividing the two levels of the green, the ball will be deflected strongly to the right.

T: Aye, the ledge goes round at almost a forty-five-degree turn, and the ground in front of the green is extremely rough.

D: That's one of the reasons it's so hard to duplicate these greens in America; you can't really produce the same conditions you find on a links course. If you have to bounce the ball in front of the green in order to stay on the putting surface, you're often in trouble on American courses. The ball may stop dead because the slope is overwatered and may not take a run-up shot. Here, if you bounce the ball far enough, you're into one of these mean pots, or you could have a hundred-yard putt – although you seldom see long putts in tournaments. What tournaments are held on this course, Tip?

If the pin is at the front, play short and bounce the ball onto the green.

T: The Dunhill Cup and the Open are the most important. I caddied for the French team a few years ago in the Dunhill Cup and we managed to beat the favorite, Australia, in the second round.

D: That shows how important the caddie is at St. Andrews.

T: The Dunhill Cup is always held in October, around the autumn equinox. During the last several years of the Cup, it was shirt sleeve weather. The pros bring their own caddies, so there's little work for the local caddies. I'm fortunate that I usually get a bag. In 1991, I caddied for Gary Player, and we only lost the final in a playoff. In a stiff breeze, this hole can be driven; in a cross breeze, ye'd also take a driver. In the typical slight summer wind from the west, like today, the professionals playing in the Dunhill Cup need a drive of about two hundred eighty yards to get to that nice flat area in the fairway.

D: That would be from the back tee. There don't seem to be any yardage makers on the Old Course. Do you know all the yardage off by heart?

T: Yes, pretty much, but I have a small notebook if I need it. The only yardages I have are from the tee to the trouble, and from the trouble to the front of the green. Very simple. I don't get complicated. With the wind, ye have to weigh it up. A lot of instinct and experience is at work. Wind plays such a major role here that ye usually have to make a judgment.

D: What about this wind? How does it affect club selection?

T: Well, today it's a one-club wind. One thing to remember about St. Andrews: Ye can play off adjacent fairways. From this hole, ye can play off the sixteenth, which parallels it. The Old Course is one of those courses where ye don't always use your own fairway.

D: Not even your own golf course, sometimes, but isn't it dangerous?

T: No, ye never hear of anyone being hit by a golf ball. Everybody's watching too carefully.

THE BUNKERS STILL DOMINATE

The Cartgate Bunker controls the strategy on this number three hole. On most of the other holes, the Old Course has a series of well-placed bunkers that dominate play. That's remarkable when you think of how much balls and clubs have changed over the years. The recent rebuilding of the tees has brought back many of the fairway bunkers into play. But the crucial bunkers guarding the greens, especially for the championship pin placements, seem to endure from one era to the next.

When over a hundred new bunkers were added to the course early in this century, the officials obviously had the Haskell ball in mind. The course was readily adapted to the new bunkers by pushing the tees back. In America, Pebble Beach and Augusta National and other mature golf courses were lengthened in a similar way. But, on the Old Course, the famous old bunkers and hazards – Cartgate, Hell, Strath, Hill, the Road, and the Valley of Sin – are still pivotal, and many a tournament has been won or lost because of them. No less a golfer than Gene Sarazen, the first man to win all four major championships, took three strokes to get out of Hill Bunker on number eleven and two to get out of Hell on number fourteen when he lost the 1934 Open Championship, and that by a single stroke. Many of the world's great golfers have won or lost a tournament at St. Andrews because of a brief flirtation, successful or otherwise, with one of the Old Course's famous hazards.

GINGER BEER
463 YARDS · PAR 4

*The green is on the right, and clearly the approach
shot does not want to go left on this hole.*

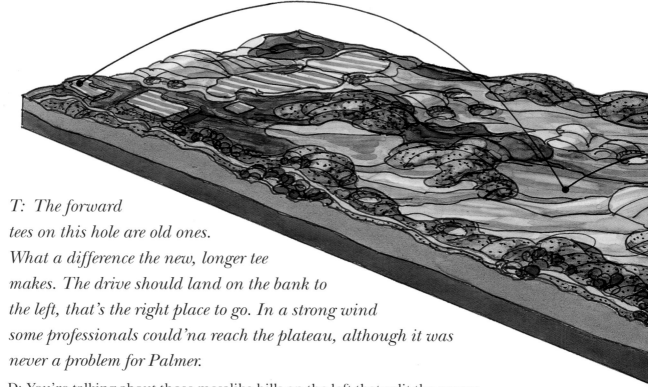

T: The forward tees on this hole are old ones. What a difference the new, longer tee makes. The drive should land on the bank to the left, that's the right place to go. In a strong wind some professionals could'na reach the plateau, although it was never a problem for Palmer.

D: You're talking about those mesalike hills on the left that split the course along fourteen and fifteen, and then make wide, enclosed valleys of four and five. The plateau has a sculptured, rolling edge, but it can be murder if you land on it, and you may lose a shot. Then, there's this little valley on the right that runs up almost dead straight toward the green.

T: Some people prefer that valley where the lies are better, especially for the Open when the pin is near the right corner of the bunker in the front middle of the green. Ye can't take the safe line when the pin is there.

D: The valley is quite narrow and shaped like a hollow; the left side is almost vertical, like a billiard table. That's visually comforting, wouldn't you say, Tip?

T: Perhaps, but ye should stay left on the wider fairway if ye can; that's definitely the way to go on this hole. From the championship tee, it's about two hundred forty yards to the ideal postion on the plateau, a long way against a slight wind, but ye should make it on a day like today. If the wind were ten miles an hour stronger, ye'd have to think (*Pointing to the tee box used by visitors*). That's at least eighty yards closer to the fairway, so your drive would be only one hundred sixty yards from there.

D: That's hard enough if you're into the wind, but the shorter carries from the forward tees certainly help the short hitter.

T: Even the short carries from the medal tees can be bad in a strong head-wind. On a more normal day, the short carries help an average golfer play any links course from the forward tees. No one can afford to get in the whins off the tee.

D: Lost balls waste time and are bad for blood pressure. There are too many places on this course for the ball to hide in the whins and tall grass-es. I understand Walter Woods once lost a truck in the tall rough while he was searching for a ball in the whins. Years ago, my friend Joe Plunket lost a horse and cart, and more. I sometimes think there are wee Scotsmen lurking in the whins who make off with your ball. I've heard that golfers have lost clubs, bags, dogs, and wives they had carefully placed in the whins while they themselves were searching for lost balls. My friend Joe Plunket found his ball, but not his wife. I heard he stopped looking for her after two days. Someone found him in the bar at Russacks muttering, "It's fate." She eventually ended up in Southern California as a bit player in a film with Groucho Marx.

T: Some people make a living finding lost golf balls on this course.

D: This number four is a very interesting, multiple choice hole. For starters, if you miss your tee shot, you're in the rough. The fairway has two arms, and the shot from the left is the more difficult. The entry to the green from this side is over a sharp mound, and the slope of the green is unsympathetic. But the fairway on the right is so very narrow you feel, as Sam Snead once said, that you have to walk single file to pass through it. It's actually about fifteen yards wide, but the green certainly looks better coming from the right side. It's a philosopher's hole; a conundrum, or, as you say in Scotland, a puzzle.

T: Ye're always in play from the left, but it's often not the best line.

D: This is a hole with a key hazard – the steep little mound in front of the green. You can see it and the flagstick from the tee. There is also a long, deep bunker across the center of the green. You certainly need to think on this hole, Tip, but, as you say, the Old Course tends to reward the well-placed shot – the one that's been well thought out.

T: Generally, it does, but if ye've a bad shot in your bag, this course will find it out.

D: The drainage seems very good all over the Old Course. You never see any puddles, even after a rainstorm.

T: It's all sand. The rainwater just goes straight down.

D: Walter Woods says the water table is one foot below the surface. My recollection of Hell Bunker years ago when I played here with my father is that it was much deeper, but perhaps that's just because I was smaller then. In any case, you don't seem to need drains here.

T: During the 1970 Open, play was suspended on the first day when an afternoon thunderstorm flooded the course. It was very similar to the rain that washed out the final round on Saturday in the 1960 Open. Arnold was angry that the afternoon round was cancelled – he thought his strength and stamina gave him an advantage playing thirty-six holes. The storm in 1970 was so bad that water rushed over the steps from the R&A Clubhouse and flooded the Valley of Sin. By the following morning, though, it was completely clear, with not a puddle to be seen. Tony Jacklin had made the turn at 29 on that first day. He had to mark his ball on the fourteenth hole when the rains hit and return the following day to complete his round.

A multiple choice driving hole, depending on conditions and shotmaking ability.

D: I remember that round. One chronicler of that Open wrote: "After the deluge, the magic was lost and Jacklin struggled to a 67." Do you think there are any other reasons why Arnold lost in 1960, other than the number of putts he took?

T: No, just his putter. I don't know why he didn't putt better. His game was solid enough. He made up for it in the next couple of years. He won the Opens at Troon and at Birkdale. As for me, of course, I was lucky enough to caddie for Tony Lema the year that Arnold didn't come, in 1964. Arnold arranged that, too, so I ended up with three Open winners and one second in five years. That's better form than I get from my horses.

D: Is this the best area for second shots up here on the plateau? You really have a wide-screen view of the green from this vantage point.

T: Aye. It's a hundred ninety-five yards from here.

D: You can see the bunkers very clearly from this spot, and in so much detail. You can also see the irritating mound in front of the green, a significant hazard that can throw off your judgment of distance. Architecturally, a good view of the green and its hazards is very useful and, I think, important. As the French-Swiss architect Le Corbusier said, "When the problem is clearly stated, the solution is at hand."

T: The bunkers don't really come into play for the professional unless it's downwind and he stupidly takes driver. Bobby Jones once drove three hundred yards into Cottage Bunker, then eagled the hole with his second. Today, it's a good four-iron shot for Arnold or anyone like him. Arnold played two clubs stronger than I did, so I just gave him two less than I would take. As I said, I would expect the pin during the championship to be toward the left side of the green.

D: So the average player would take at least a two iron if he got this far? That would mean that the mound in front of the green would be very much in play. In a strong headwind, this would be true even for the professional. Was the bunker on the left added, or is it original?

T: I believe it's original.

D: The second, third, and fourth holes all have a bunker in front of the middle part of the green, and in each case, the pin can be put near the bunker or behind it to make the hole very tough. This is especially true on a long par four like this.

T: This is a long hole today, all right. This fourth hole was recorded at the last Open Championship as the most difficult. It's such an easy green to three putt. And, if the wind was blowing any stronger, ye'd have a hard time getting up here on this plateau – just getting home in two would be a task in itself.

The Cottage Bunker is not usually in play, but if you have one bad shot in your bag, it will find this difficult bunker.

D: With the prevailing wind coming across from left to right, you would have to allow for the ball landing on these hard greens at an angle, and running. Do you have any rules for that?

T: Yes. If ye allow ten yards for the wind and ten yards for the run, ye'd aim twenty yards left of the flag, instead of ten.

D: I guess the ball runs so much because the green slopes left to right, back to the Ginger Beer Bunker, and is therefore receptive to a draw from the narrow fairway on the right.

T: That's true, but the green is very hard because it's dried out from the wind. Ye won't see any ball marks on the green. That's solid sand underneath the grass, and very firm.

D: With this wind against, Tip, you'd need a shorter, much tighter swing to keep the ball down and make it run. A lazy hook will bore into the wind, but with a fade, you can lose the shot. On one's first visit to St. Andrews, that's not an easy judgment. What about the shot when it's downwind?

T: Whether downwind or with the wind from the south, the narrow fairway is more of a risk, so ye go left. It's a large green, with some funny little slopes. The pin is always to the left for tournaments, but to the right for regular play, so there is plenty of green to work with on the second shot.

D: Most of this green runs into the fairway, a bit like number ten, and is flat with smallish rolls, but look at that undulating stretch of green at the back right. Has that been added?

T: Aye, it was never there before, and it's never used except in winter. The pin is always over there, near the bunker, and that's where it'll be next week for the St. Andrews Trophy. The pin would never be on the right during a championship.

D: That championship pin position looks about a hundred fifty feet from the right edge of the green and definitely brings the bunker into play. Is the pin position restricted to that area of the green during the championship?

T: Yes, it might be back a bit, but certainly there will never be more than twenty percent of the green used.

D: There are about six thousand square feet in this relatively small area alone, which is bigger than the average American green. Apart from that, the double green must be about forty thousand square feet, all told, which is almost an acre. That area on the far right of the green is a real roller coaster. Nobody would enjoy putting over all these rolls; they're really unreasonable.

T: They had the pin down there last week, but I agree, it's Mickey Mouse.

D: Those are fifteen, maybe twenty percent grades. The ball will just keep rolling and stop in a hollow. On the other hand, nobody, apart from touring professionals, expects golf or life to be totally reasonable. The mound on the green side, to the windward, is higher than the regular bunker. As I explained before, mounds are built up by sand blown by the wind, and by golfers hitting sand shots toward the green. The features around a green can change several feet in elevation over a period of years. These ridges we see, which were not

WORTHY OF A
LIFETIME'S STUDY

Excluding the Swilcan Burn on number one, which is certainly formidable, I've always found the first four holes on the Old Course the most conventional of the eighteen. This is also true of the starting holes at other famous courses; I'm thinking specifically of Augusta National and Pebble Beach. The golfer needs time to fold himself into the round, and he's much more prepared for drama after he's played some straightforward golf the first few holes. He has a better chance to get going, as it were, if the more memorable holes occur later in the round. That doesn't mean that these holes can't be subtle, like the third at Pebble Beach, or exacting like this fourth on the Old Course. But, great holes should demand at least one and possibly two daring shots to achieve a birdie, with harsh penalties provided for any rash adventurism that doesn't come off. Such holes should be well anchored in the body of the round to allow a golfer to establish his tempo, rhythm, and confidence by the time he reaches them.

The irritating mound in front of the green can throw off judgement of the correct distance.

there originally, make the greens semiblind. Bunkers like this are never designed by an architect. They are a product of nature, although the members think they've always been there. This is also true of features at Pebble Beach, Riviera, and many of the older American golf courses. I know these bunkers didn't always have sharply defined edges, did they?

T: No. They were a lot tougher years ago.

D: The edges must have been easier to maintain then, and much more attractive. Perhaps they looked more natural, but golfers could land in some impossible lies with those rough edges. Some new courses in America have artificially made ragged edges. Is there any suggestion of going back to the older ways?

T: No! These cleaner edges are better for golf.

D: Perhaps some people feel that ragged edges would make the course look unkempt by modern standards, and with all this play, it might. I understand that most visitors from afar, especially Americans, find the appearance of the fairways slightly strange. Sam Snead thought St. Andrews was an old abandoned golf course when he first saw it in 1946 while riding the train from Leuchars. As we know, he won that Open.

T: Quite often, all of the grass turns brown through lack of rain and the place looks pretty tired. Even then, it plays wonderfully well. It's just a look most visitors aren't used to. Sometimes, the only green parts of the course are the greens themselves.

D: This hole must be over four hundred fifty yards from the championship tee, to a huge green – a three-, or even a four-club green, as they might say.

T: The difficulty is in getting the pace of the putt. The toughest pin position is behind the front bunker, because ye can't see the hole from just behind it.

D: There's another tough pin position on the other side, nipping at the waist of the greens. Surely, you shouldn't put the pin at the waist; that's really laying it on.

T: People do get into the Ginger Beer Bunker behind the green, but not too often.

D: The green is about two hundred feet wide at this point; this is where you'd be apt to risk taking three putts, and perhaps be grateful for only three. You can see the bents coming through here. They are a darker green and have a flatter blade than the fescues. I can also see patches of *Poa annua*, which is light green and irregular; still, the green is amazingly true. Sometimes, the distance is hard to judge, but the line is always true – as true as any I know of.

T: Unless ye can see an absolute, definite borrow – what Americans call break – most putts on the Old Course are going to the straight. There are great rolls and humps on the greens, it's true, but near the cups, the surface is very flat and even. Ye can't be timid on these greens.

D: These putting surfaces show that the American obsession with having the same strain of grass on all greens – monoculture – is unreasonable. Walter says the golfers here learn to make allowances for the *Poa*, and he encourages it to fill out the greens. Look at Olympic in San Francisco – the entire course is *Poa annua*, considered a bad weed grass in America. Yet, at Olympic and most of the courses on the Monterey Peninsula, the greens, tees, and fairways are all composed of this supposedly noxious, inconsistent turf, and it works just fine. That's true also at Jasper and Banff in the Canadian Rockies where they use rye grass, which is also found here at St. Andrews.

T: The different grasses on the St. Andrews greens have always seemed strange to golfers from other countries.

SEQUENCE, RHYTHM, AND CHARACTER

After you've played the first four holes, it's rather easy to picture the Old Course in the role of a patriarch who makes the rules and then proceeds to break them if he feels like it. Yet, nobody familiar with this course can fail to notice the excellence and consistency of the sequence and rhythm of its holes. There are no holdups, no par threes or fivess to slow up play in the first four holes, in fact, no par threes until number eight. The Old Course is a blueprint for the new Pace fast play system pioneered by the USGA and my friend William Yates.

After a relatively soft start, the Old Course strikes a fine balance between open and closed holes, between those with whins and those without, between long and short, difficult and easy holes. The intriguing mix continues with flat holes and those with irregular, rolling fairways; holes that look bland and those that excite from the tee; single greens and double greens; bunkers galore, of various shapes, sizes, and depths. These contrasting elements are masterfully synthesized and choreographed. No single person could possibly learn all the details of the Old Course short of a lifetime of study, and perhaps not even then.

Within its rhythms and sequence of holes, the combinations of golfing possibilities are virtually infinite. And who can predict the wind, which varies mightily in force, consistency, and duration? Only a caddie or a long-time member can read the wind with any confidence.

But no one, I am convinced, will ever know where all the humps, hollows, ridges, deflecting mounds, and hidden pockets are located.

HOLE O'CROSS

564 YARDS · PAR 5

It is imperative to play left on this hole, as can be seen from this view of the whins in the foreground.

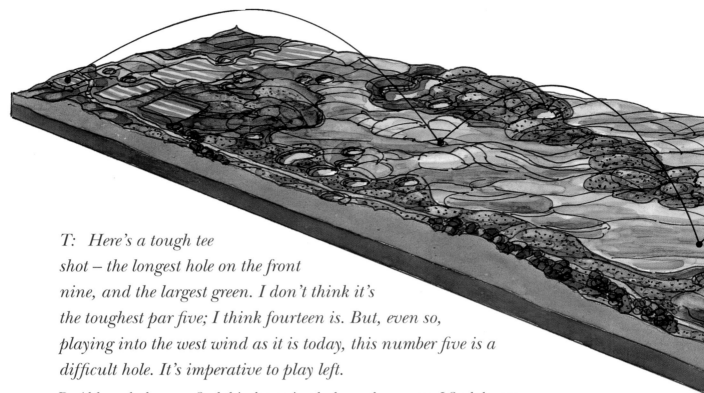

T: Here's a tough tee
shot – the longest hole on the front
nine, and the largest green. I don't think it's
the toughest par five; I think fourteen is. But, even so,
playing into the west wind as it is today, this number five is a
difficult hole. It's imperative to play left.

D: Although the pros find this the easiest hole on the course, I find the tee shot intimidating. All you can see are shaggy mounds ahead. You can't help but notice the fourteenth hole, which parallels this one and has lots of character. These shared fairways work on your mind. Here we are, walking along five and thinking about fourteen. It's an interesting bit of trivia that these parallel fairways always add up to nineteen, but the joined greens to eighteen.

T: Fourteen does have character. A plateau'd fairway. The Beardies Bunkers, Hell Bunker, a difficult green *and* out of bounds. On this fifth hole, ye must go left; and I've said that before, haven't I? Well, it's a general rule of the Old Course, which favors a hooker except for holes nine and ten.

D: And number two.

T: Yes, that's right. Here on Hole O'Cross are several bunkers on the direct line up the right side – the Seven Sisters, they're called. If ye get in one of them, ye'll be playing out backwards or sideways because ye can't go forward, and there's a shot lost. Those bunkers are two hundred twenty to two hundred sixty yards out, so ye've got to go way left – almost fifty yards – to be safe.

D: I heard that Nicklaus hit the bunkers three times in the 1964 Open, even though he drove farther left each time. He failed to realize that the little valleys in the fairways guide balls into the bunkers.

T: Yes, I told Lema to hit it left, and he avoided them all. But, ye must be careful; if ye're wild enough, ye may reach Hell Bunker from the tee. I once caddied for Phil Rodgers in a television match, and he knocked it in there for the publicity.

D: In Hell?

T: Aye. Mind ye, he was drunk the night before. He had two wives and six kids to go home to. He started off with Guinness; I left at eight o'clock that night, but he was still there at closing. He could really put it away, yet he almost won two Opens. They were sports in those days, not so serious as they are now.

D: Yes, we've almost forgotten that golf is a game, not a religion or a business deal.

T: There are too many who would disagree.

D: This small tree is a hawthorn. There are trees on the St. Andrews links, in spite of what the books say. I've noticed sycamores, maples, and Swedish white beam, as well as hawthorns mixed in with the whins, or gorse. Obviously, you could have tree-lined fairways here, but I don't think anybody would like them. Somehow, trees and links are antonymic. In this exposed location, the trees would be small and wind-warped. Scale on the linksland comes from the gorse, not from trees. This is a great scene with those fine, high clumps of flowering gorse off to the north. They're actually on the New Course, but the change in scale is dramatic and uplifting with all those masses of yellow blossoms, and later on when the heather turns purple.

T: It can hurt to play out of the heather, especially when it's in bloom.

D: I don't like heather for golf. It's like playing off steel wool.

T: Ye ca'na break the stems, so ye must try to pick the ball off the body of the plant. Better to stay out of it. On this hole, the pros would hit into some of these undulations in the fairway. If they can hit to the survey stone, near the Pulpit Bunker, there's no problem to get home.

D: That's an ominous description of a bunker, even the name makes you feel tight and constricted (*Standing near the two bunkers before the green*).

T: Aye. Ye could'na get it near the ridge today; ye'd have to hit a five or six iron, and lay up from back there at the landing area. If ye get in either of these two parallel bunkers set into the slope in front of the green, it's dead-

The two bunkers are stragetically placed to punish faulty shots. The professionals will carry over them, the average golfer should play short.

ly. They are similar to the Spectacle Bunkers at Carnoustie, but these on the Old Course don't really have a name.

D: They do seem to stare at you, though, as you walk down the fairway. Into a headwind, the pros would have to wonder about reaching the green in two. What about today, Tip?

T: There's nae advantage in trying today because there's nae chance to get home against this wind. Something like a five iron would be the ideal club for the second, which would leave a shot of about one hundred twenty yards to the hole.

D: Where would you lay up? In the middle?

T: Aye, no' too close to the bunkers.

D: I guess the worst thing you can do in trying to lay up is to knock it into one of the bunkers. In America, we often face the same situation if there's water in the landing area. You must be careful in a following wind, too. The fairway narrows as the ridge closes in. You'd have to be very accurate with your drive to get any advantage from a following wind on this hole. (*Standing at the plateau before the green*) You look at this, and think it's the green.

T: The big thing here is that ye don't realize how far these bunkers are from the front of the green.

D: Very hard to judge, I'd say, but whatever the distance may be, there's an illusion here, which makes this the most deceptive hole on the course, at least for the first-time player, because he thinks the green is just behind the bunkers. This is what makes it a fascinating hole. If it weren't for that, it would be just another straightforward, long par five.

T: If ye stand up here above the bunkers, ye can see the plateau coming right round here.

D: The plateau's about twenty yards long, and then there's a dip thirty yards wide, and beyond it this huge green. The plateau and the green merge into each other visually, making the green appear even bigger. The grand illusion. The dip is actually an irregular canyon formed by the plateau'd green and is perhaps seven feet below its crown. The ground there is rough, with broken little slopes; standing there, the green above you seems endless. There's a sense of eternal space just here, and you can really smell the fresh air.

T: Aye. Ye may have a wedge from behind these spectacle bunkers after ye lay up, or as much as a five iron, depending on the wind. Normally, it's an eight or nine iron to get home.

D: With a following wind, I suppose you would want to take enough club to avoid being taken in by the illusion – what some might say is the choice

A closeup view of the two pot bunkers that can do serious damage.

between a short pitch or a long putt. What's interesting to me about this hole is that it's really a two-level golf course at this point.

T: Aye. The Elysian Fields of the fourteenth hole are much higher than the fifth fairway, where we're standing now.

D: The fairway on the lower level keeps going, and then runs into a steep grass wall of long rough and gorse, which encircles the plateau'd green on three sides, raising it to the level of the fourteenth fairway and, spatially, borrowing on it. This green is bigger than the landing area of the average par four hole. Surely, there could be five clubs difference on shots to this green, Tip?

T: It could be five clubs, anyway.

D: Is there much variation on the placement of the pin?

T: It's always placed in the right side, and mostly forward, to keep this hole separate from number thirteen's.

D: With greens this big, you can use a relatively small area for the pin positions without wearing out the surface. How does the hole play if the pin is at the back?

T: Very long; at fifteen yards from the back, it's nearly six hundred yards. One and two-thirds acres in area – that's seventy thousand square feet. You might have a putt of well over a hundred *yards* on this green. How's that for a Texas wedge? You could play football on it, or even baseball. Chop it up, and you'd have eighteen greens each of about four thousand square feet.

For comparison, greens in America average about five thousand square feet. You could get ten full-sized tennis courts on this green. You could even play Centrifugal Bumble Puppy.

T: What's that?

D: A game invented by Aldous Huxley in his novel *Antic Hay*. I played the left bumble position, but only as an alternate.

T: Some people chip here, but that's discouraged by the management.

D: You don't have to take a divot; I believe Gary Player has chipped on this green, and afterwards there were complaints. When you arrive on top of the green, it's actually rather flat, with three long rolls on the left and three shallower rolls in the center.

T: Most people are surprised when they find only two par fives on the Old Course, but then there are only two par threes, as well.

Never go left to approach this green, which is otherwise relatively flat and reasonable.

HALLOWED GROUND

On the green, one has a sense of being in a bowl surrounded by broad splashes of brilliant, yellow gorse under a ridge of purplish hills, an effective composition both in form and color. Behind the Old Town are several banded fields of bright, mustard-colored oil-rape plants, and, beyond them, rounded, tree-crested hills low on the horizon. Halfway along number five fairway and from the sixth tee onward, the Old Course seems to change pace. The fairways merge not only among themselves but also with the New Course, and, to a lesser extent, with the Eden. Finally, around the eleventh and twelfth holes, the combined courses seem to fan out across the estuary to embrace the entire north of Scotland.

Out here among the gorse and sand grass, there is a festivity of fresh air and wind. The golfer is apt to feel more vulnerable if he's playing badly, but more triumphant if playing well. The surrounding countryside in turn greets and touches the Old Course as it stretches out along its peninsula toward the Eden River. Out here, the wind is keener and has great speed, as it always does when traveling unimpeded over water. Pockets of air swoop down, bouncing off the blossoming gorse, sometimes pushing the ball in unexpected directions before finally ricocheting back to the canopy of sky.

On a spring day, when the wind is light and the sun is shining, the greens, the rough, the fairways, and the cavalcade of gorse that frames the distant fields combine with the sea and calico hills to strike a chord of simple, natural beauty, one that I have not seen duplicated in my travels in over a hundred countries. At times like this, especially, the Old Course is hallowed ground, indeed, worthy of pilgrimage. In such a setting, a golfer can concentrate on his game with a song in his heart. He may sense the myth surrounding the place and the ghosts that resonate through all the centuries since the Old Course and the ancient links first found each other. He might hear, too, echoes of the eager peals of laughter and muttered curses generated so often in this place by the tantalizing, maddening, solitary, exhilarating, fraternal, mortifying, yet rewarding game that gave it birth.

HEATHERY

416 YARDS · PAR 4

The depth of the green allows the approach
shot to hold, even with a following wind.

*T: It's a
driver here, and then perhaps a nine iron or a wedge. Ye
might need a longer iron if ye're an average
golfer or if ye're into wind. Ye have to get the correct
line for the drive, that's the key to this hole. Ye can see a white
marker post up there on the hill, in front of the tee. Today, ye'd
want to hit your drive about ten yards left of the marker. It's one of
those holes where ye think there's plenty of room, but ye've only to
hit it slightly off line to find the bunkers on the right side. There are
four of them, almost two hundred forty to two hundred eighty yards
out. If ye go over the hill too far to the left side, ye'll be into the
Coffins, which are only slightly nearer the tee, though they're really
hazards for the thirteenth hole.*

D: This championship tee looks new, Tip. How long has it been here?

T: Maybe thirty years.

D: That's definitely new for St. Andrews. This is a pretty depressing view
from the tee, Tip, one of the most formidable you could encounter. Directly
in front are large mounds of gorse eight to ten feet tall, heaving and tossing
as if the earth were ready to erupt. You could easily be lost in the tangled
foliage and knee-high grasses that choke the hollows and valleys. It must be
terrifying to the first-time golfer.

T: If ye walk forward along the tee, ye can see the hole is not as bad as it
looks from the championship tee, and ye can see the direction better.

D: From the tournament tee, you're actually playing over the edge of the fifth green, then?

T: Aye. This tee was once part of the green, but it's a large one – over one and a half acres in area. Years ago, the rules required players to tee their balls within two club lengths of the hole, but that was very hard on the green. The holes were seldom moved. After holing out, the golfer would reach in the hole for a handful of sand to make a tee. Soon, the holes were so deep players could'na retrieve the ball. Old Tom Morris selected the iron marker from which the iron cups were made to stabilize the holes, and eventually the greens were made bigger and separate tees constructed. From the medal tee, the white marker is the perfect line, but from the forward tee, ye'd want to hit left of the marker.

D: From the back tees, the white marker itself is the correct target?

T: Yes, otherwise the shot's blind.

D: It is sometimes hard to know where to go next on this course. Unless you have a caddie, you could easily get lost and wind up playing on one of the other courses, Eden or Jubilee, as visitors sometimes do.

T: Yes, some Japanese golfers have come back to the clubhouse wondering why they played nineteen or twenty-one holes, instead of eighteen.

D: Maybe that's because the Japanese don't like boundaries. I guess you could easily play holes from three different courses if you weren't careful.

T: Some people play out on the Old and come back on the New.

D: Number six hole is the beginning of a group of similar holes. This is the principle of the rhythmic grouping of easy and hard holes on golf courses like Merion in Philadelphia, and the contrasts of the seaside and inland holes at Pebble Beach. Those were laid out by man. I wonder if it was accidental here, or intentional?

T: I think it probably just happened. The loop really starts at number
seven, but from six through twelve, the pros have got to score. Six, seven,
eight, nine, and ten, especially, are the scoring holes; they've got to make
their birdies there. That's where Tony Lema won the Open. In the second
round, he went from number six through thirteen in level threes. In the
third round, Nicklaus was on the twelfth when Lema was on the sixth, the
green alongside. They could watch each other drive off. Nicklaus was then
only one stroke behind, but Lema went the next eight holes in one over
threes, and built his lead to seven up by the end of the round. On the last
round, Lema was two over. He had only twenty-seven holes of practice
before the Open. I said: "That's not enough around here." He said: "Tell
me where to hit it, Tip, and I will hit it there."

*Bunkers on the left,
bunkers on the
right. It's best to hit
the drive straight
down the middle.*

D: Lema's victory after seeing the course for the first time only days before has to be one of the great feats of tournament golf.

T: It certainly amazed me.

D: He couldn't have done it without you, Tip. He was the horse, you were the jockey. Maybe you both should have won the cup.

T: No' many people see it that way, although I have to say that Lema did.

D: Once you get to the landing area, this hole is not so bad; the average player does have a fair chance. Out here, the fairway seems continuous and there's little of that violent rough we saw from the tee – at least, not until you reach the Eden River. This fairway is rather flat, yet the environs are full of character and movement. But, you are likely to breathe a sigh of relief on reaching the landing area. This is another spot where St. Andrews reaches out to the natural world. The sense of space is limitless. The escape from bricks and concrete is complete, a welcome release for those who perhaps only hours before have left the city. Finding an expanse of space is one of the hallowed traditions of golf that so many modern architects have virtually ignored.

T: Ye get a pretty good lie on this fairway, and there's plenty of room.

D: The contrast is so strong from tee to landing area. The war and peace theme, again. From the golfer's point of view, it's upsetting and liberating at the same time. This is a friendly fairway – another one, like number twelve, with deep bunkers that are essentially blind from the tee because the Old Course was once played in the opposite direction.

T: Aye, the reverse course. They played it from the present greens to the present tees. I did, once, when I was fairly young. It was all right, but no' quite as interesting as the regular course.

D: This little bunker in between the sixth and fourteenth fairways keeps catching shots. Some of these blind bunkers are really large, and there's not much room between them, either.

T: Ye must go either left or right of them. Professionals do okay here unless there's a big wind, but amateurs have a hard time.

D: Faldo doesn't often get in bunkers, but he's been in the Coffins on the left side of this fairway. You can see the bunkers clearly enough if you look from the green toward the tee, as we said.

T: Maybe. They're certainly invisible going this way. From the tee, ye're just guessing, and if ye're downwind, ye musn't go left or ye'll surely be in them – although the pros today probably can hit far enough to stay out of the trouble.

Once the drive reaches the landing area, the rest of the fairway to the green is open and very fair.

D: These high ridges in the fairway make judging distances very difficult, which is another factor in playing at St. Andrews. Once again, it proves you need a good caddie.

T: Aye. There's no background to many of the holes. Experience really helps in judging the distances.

D: The gorse in bloom – some would say the blooming gorse – also helps a great deal because it provides a frame. How would you play your second shot on this hole, Tip? Can you go for a pitch and run? The ground undulates a bit in the landing area, but the lies are good and the green is wide and fairly deep at this end of the double-green.

T: Aye, it's a wedge from where we're standing. But if ye want to run it up, ye'd use a seven or eight iron; ye'd run it through this little valley here. Most of the pros prefer the wedge because they don't want to take a chance on the bounce.

D: There's an irregular ridge in front of the green, followed by a miniature Valley of Sin. You can't see the bottom of the flagstick, and another valley runs across the middle of the green, so you may have trouble holding the green. At least there are no bunkers to worry about. The approach shot will need plenty of backspin, wouldn't you say, Tip?

T: Aye, if ye use the wedge. The green has been enlarged, and when the pin's on the right, ye can see the flagstick. The green cuts wider around the outside, but it's a much bigger target than twelve, the adjoining green. Twelve is really narrow.

D: Surely even at St. Andrews they wouldn't put the flag down at this lower level, with all these bumps?

T: Yes, they would. They'll put the hole anywhere on the green because of the increased volume of play. In some ways, it is more normal to have it down below.

D: Just another of the eccentricities of St. Andrews, I suppose, but the depth in the green allows you to hold in a following wind.

T: Aye, this is one of the easier holes if ye're playing the wind.

INTO THE WILDERNESS

Here, for the first time, you enter into an intimate relationship with the far shore of the Eden River. This is your first sight of water, and from this hole onwards for several more, water becomes a visual part of the course. The gorse here is in well-formed clumps whose shapes and forms across the tops of the mounds resemble those of the distant hills. As you travel outward and the town recedes, you feel as if you're entering uncharted ground. Out toward the Eden Estuary, golfers visiting for the first time tend to lose their bearings and sense of orientation.

From the seventh hole on, as you cross back upon yourself and then begin to return to greens already visited, you really must pay attention to where you're going or risk becoming confused. Away from the town and civilization, golfers find a wild, windy, flat ground cast beneath the infinite space and horizon of the North Sea, with miles of trudging against a cold, penetrating wind before any refuge comes into view. When the trees are in bloom against the distant escarpment, the scene has a luminous, singing beauty, but there's a peculiarly Scottish sense of melancholy and forboding, too. Nature, like the Old Course itself, reminds us of both glory and mortality.

HIGH

372 YARDS · PAR 4

Spectators like to sit patiently and watch the players'
struggles on this slight dogleg, one of two on the course.

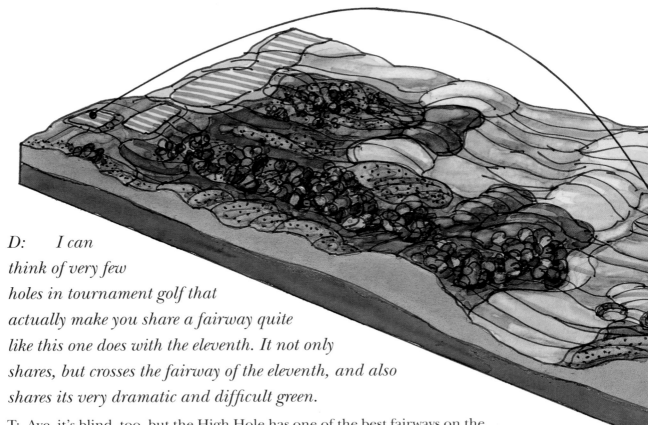

*D: I can
think of very few
holes in tournament golf that
actually make you share a fairway quite
like this one does with the eleventh. It not only
shares, but crosses the fairway of the eleventh, and also
shares its very dramatic and difficult green.*

T: Aye, it's blind, too, but the High Hole has one of the best fairways on the course, if ye can find it. The rough and whins are to the right. Ye must drive along their edge into the valley of the fairway shared by the two holes, then ye're almost home. There's only a wedge or nine iron left, and the green is no problem. I agree, though, it's an odd sort of hole. The green for this hole's on the wrong side of the double green, and that's uncomfortable. The big Cockle Bunker is hidden from the tee, and the pros will sometimes hit a one iron to avoid it. This is a slight dogleg to the right; we don't have any other holes at St. Andrews with real doglegs, ye know, except perhaps the seventeenth.

D: What an imposing view looking backward from the tee! And, what a wild scene it is looking toward the green, to the northwest, I believe – a shot into the great unknown. A first-time golfer could scarcely imagine what he's hitting into; Paradise Lost, perhaps. The small, thick, rolling hills near the tee have terrific mass and void. They're rather like the foothills of the Himalayas. I heard one man was lost here for three days; he was eventually found in the bar of the Gleneagles Hotel. Last year, I understand they caught an Italian prisoner of war who'd been hiding in these hills for fifty-one years.

T: They do roll quite a bit.

D: These hills have a deceptive scale. They exude raw power and seem much bigger than they are. There's an enormous store of natural energy trapped in them. These hills tend to stay stubbornly in the mind until they are met again coming back on the thirteenth.

T: The high handicapper can shoot right toward the red flag on the eleventh green, or at the hill behind it that joins the seventh green. If ye keep to the left, there are no bunkers to worry about, and even though your second shot will be longer, ye won't have to hit over Cockle. Some average golfers can really hit the ball, they just can't score. A full drive from a long hitter could land in Cockle Bunker, but that's unlikely if ye're into the prevailing wind.

D: As you come over this rise, you can see the whole green with its lovely, wide fairway and the bunkers in front. I suppose it's Paradise Regained. The mounds to the left are well shaped, and there's a large, well-articulated depression to the right. Everything looks natural. A modern shaper would have a hard time getting the grades that good, although Harry Colt produced some fine forms on the Eden Course before they started changing it.

T: None of us like what they've done to the Eden. Even if Cockle is well in front of the green, it's about the biggest bunker on the course.

D: Yes, Cockle Bunker has the same monumental quality as a Cezanne painting, or those hills we just passed off the tee. Cockle is forty yards across, ten yards wide, and nine or ten feet deep. That's over three thousand square feet of bunker – bigger than the old fifth green at Pebble Beach. Because of its monumentality, Cockle feels much bigger than it actually is, and the volume it controls is substantial because the front face is near vertical. At this moment, a few dandelion, yarrow, and other weeds grow from the grass "bricks" that form its side, but otherwise this wall of turf is as long and solid as the base of a medieval castle. Cockle Bunker appears to be alive with an almost insolent, visual ferocity; it really stares you down. Cockle is a bunker's bunker.

T: Good players don't often get in Cockle.

D: It's pretty frightening for the handicap golfer. And so, at times, is the little trip round the corner of this fairway, straight into the shooting gallery of golf balls being hit from the adjacent eleventh tee.

T: The carry is well over two hundred yards – maybe two hundred twenty from the back tee.

D: You can see how this double-green was plateau'd, a grand creation by Old Tom Morris. Who says that nature built St. Andrews? The fine, sculptural monumentality of this man-made green is a legacy to golf course architects everywhere. It's one of the first designed by man, rather than found by

Locate the tee from the drawing, and you can see that this is a formidable driving hole. The green is on the left, behind ten-foot-deep Cockle Bunker.

The plateau'd double green was created by Old Tom Morris as an addition to the original natural links.

him. This green couldn't have been better fitted into the total structure of the hole even if it had been part of the original links, which it wasn't.

T: The second shot is hard, unless the wind is slightly against. Ye must get the ball on the green.

D: It's an amazing creation. The main slope is left to right, but there are other slopes, some front to back. What would you do, Tip? Take your chances with a pitch to the left near the Strath Bunker, or come in from the right, over it, hoping for an uphill putt? Even as you walk up to this green, you feel your stomach tightening.

T: The ball will deflect right when it hits the green. Ye can take your preference today of how ye'll play, but on more normal days when the hole plays into the prevailing west crosswind, ye'd have to be well to the left with your wedge.

D: Would you flatten the blade and keep it low?

T: Ye never want it too high in a wind.

D: Standing on the green, you can see the entire estuary with the hills behind and, beyond the back slope, the lyme grass that was planted to hold the banks in the last century. When the green's exposed like this, the wind has to affect the putts.

T: Aye, ye have to allow for borrow and wind even more than usual. The seventh, eleventh, and twelfth greens are more exposed than any others on the course, as they back up to the Eden River. Play has been stopped in tournaments when the ball may move on the green from the force of the wind. Because of this, Walter Woods cuts the seventh/eleventh green slightly higher.

D: I noticed at the 1995 Open that balls were stopping on that steep slope above Strath Bunker at number eleven. Walter must have had the grass at a speed of about seven or eight on the Stimp meter.

T: Anyway, they were slow enough to hold the ball.

HISTORIC BUNKERS AND STRATEGY

On hole number three, we discussed the significance of the hazards on the Old Course, and the durability of the location of the key bunkers. This seventh/eleventh hole is a fine example of Old Course bunkering. You don't have to be an architect to appreciate the stern character and compressed energy of these bunkers, their seemingly perfect placement, the sense of inevitability they give off, and their mystic power. These bunkers, especially the Road and the Strath, act like magnets for loose balls. The center of the seventeenth green pours into the Road Bunker, and even balls landing on the slope below the green will trickle back into the sand. Hill Bunker here on seven/eleven will also gather balls into its grainy depths, and it's deeper and more difficult than the Road Bunker. Tip always says darkly that this bunker was actually the crater left by a bomb dropped in World War II.

The key bunkers on the Old Course have an authority and presence, and many are named. One can't help surmising that Strath, Hill, Hell, and Lions Mouth have been crafted as carefully as a great opera or a ballet. One has a feeling at the Old Course of masterful scale and rightness in the rhythm and sequence of bunkers, a sense that many were placed there not by the Almighty or nature, but by some long forgotten intelligence. Change is inevitable on golf courses, but it's usually slow and incremental, and hardly noticed. When the members of a club say they want their golf course restored to its original design, I've found they usually want to go back fifteen years, not fifty. At St. Andrews, the changes have been occurring for a few hundred years and have become embedded in time, polished by the patina of tradition.

One cannot help believing, too, that the famous old University, one of the oldest and best in the world, has played a part in this and that the Old Course has been a beneficiary of its faculty and students. The placement and refinement of the hazards have been a fortunate legacy of the ideas from the minds of its golfer scholars. Over the centuries, these men, through their critical recommendations, have done their part in bringing the course to its present unique standard of strategy, to the eternal benefit of everybody who has lifted a club on this venerable stage.

SHORT

178 YARDS · PAR 3

*Looking back toward the tee from
the eighth green (on the right).*

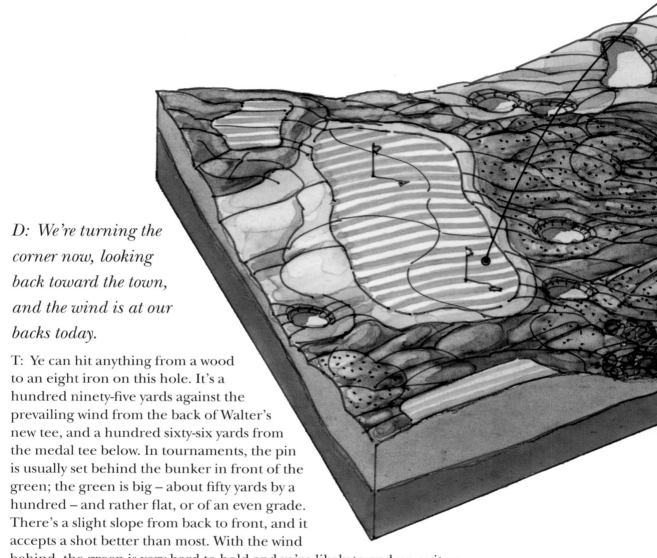

D: We're turning the corner now, looking back toward the town, and the wind is at our backs today.

T: Ye can hit anything from a wood to an eight iron on this hole. It's a hundred ninety-five yards against the prevailing wind from the back of Walter's new tee, and a hundred sixty-six yards from the medal tee below. In tournaments, the pin is usually set behind the bunker in front of the green; the green is big – about fifty yards by a hundred – and rather flat, or of an even grade. There's a slight slope from back to front, and it accepts a shot better than most. With the wind behind, the green is very hard to hold and ye're likely to end up quite a long way past the hole, or even off the green. This green joins with number ten, so ye can see the tenth flag as ye putt out on number eight. Frankly, I like the puzzle from the shorter tee.

D: It's a formidable hole from this new tee. We know that the higher you are, the more wind you have to combat. Up here, on this higher tee, you can see everything before you – the huge green with its pervasive sense of endless flatness – just as you can at the tiny Postage Stamp at Troon.

T: None of us like this new tee.

D: My complaint would be that the surface of the tee is not big enough. Otherwise, I have to admit that I like it. As an architect, I like the symbolic power you get from hitting off higher tees and the better view it offers of the target. You're no longer in the pits; you're king of the castle. Conservatives might not like to hear this, but nearly every inland golf course in the world would benefit from raising most of its tees by three to six feet, or more. This is part of the so-called loop, isn't it?

T: Aye, this and the next two holes are the easiest on the course and are bound to help your card.

D: People tend to be critical of this eighth hole. They call it simple, another semiblind par three, but if you're playing with the prevailing southwest wind behind, this hole can be a terror for the average golfer. Judgment is crucial here. I've seen John Daly hit it straight over the green. Many pros aim their shots just over the bunker, and the following wind blows them off the back of the green.

T: Well, that's true, it can be difficult. Even for the professional, the caddie must give him the right club if there's a wind.

D: From the new back tee, I think this hole is much harder, but also more interesting. Personally, I think this tee adds backbone, although the hole already had a peculiar mood of its own. On the left side is a mean web of gorse and rough, which tends to give the hole closure. The foreground is filled with rolls of thick, matted grass and heather that run right up to the putting surface. The great depth of the green gives golfers a sporting chance on this mainly downwind hole. Most of the time, the pin's behind the front bunker, which is six feet deep and ten across. The green slopes back steeply from the bunker to the tournament pin position, and it's hard to hold a shot just there. A big hump at the top of the bunker makes the green semiblind. When I helped remodel some of the holes at Pebble Beach for the 1992 US Open, I noticed several greens were semiblind because of humps above the greenside bunkers, formed by golfers hitting sand up into the wind. The slope behind this bunker at number eight is formed in exactly the same way, by windblown sand. These big bunker lips are not architectural, then, but organic, and they can give a hole character. What do you think, Tip?

T: Well, it's certainly some bunker, but it's several yards short of the green. There's another bunker hidden in that depression on the right. Ye don't notice it unless ye're in it. The green is very wide, and ye can easily take too little club. That's the key here – keep the ball straight, and choose the right club.

D: Everybody who has ever visited St. Andrews talks about playing the wind. The Scots say, "If there's nae wind and nae weather, there's nae gawf."

T: Yes, this eighth hole is a different proposition without wind.

You can hit anything from a wood to an eight iron on this par three, depending on the wind.

Thick, matted grass and heather run right up to the green.

PLAYING THE WIND

The wind makes the dunes, which form the links; those who play the links play the wind, and those who play the wind tend to favor a hook or a draw. A drawn shot will bore into the wind, whereas a fade tends to be carried away by it. In the early days of golf in America, many of its better golfers – though not all – played with a hook, or draw, which they had learned from the immigrant Scottish professionals who brought the game, and their swings, to America. But they didn't bring the wind.

As time passed, golf in America developed on inland, tree-lined courses that were largely sheltered from wind. A fade or even a slice, some golfers believed, was easier to control than a hook. Lee Trevino, a natural hooker who switched to the fade, says: "You can talk to a fade, but a hook won't listen." After his near-fatal car accident, Ben Hogan changed his natural hook to a conscious left-to-right shot pattern that he called a power fade, and his theories influenced play in America. Jack Nicklaus as a teenager had a natural draw, which his excellent teacher Jack Grout converted to a fade.

Nicklaus became the world's best player using this shape of shot. Arnold Palmer, on the other hand, was one of those who retained his natural hook, and, though somewhat wild as a youngster, later became one of the greatest drivers in the game.

Although the top players can fade or draw to order, certain courses favor players who play with a natural hook, and the Old Course is one of these. So is the Augusta National, with eleven holes that dogleg from right to left. It is no surprise, then, when we recall that Palmer, Sam Snead, Seve Ballesteros, Bobby Jones, and even Jack Nicklaus have always played well on these two golf courses. Nicklaus is a better wind player than he admits. Grout taught him to hit high approaches under normal conditions, which had little roll after landing. Downwind, Jack still hits them high, but takes one or two clubs less than normal. He hits hard to get the ball as high as possible so that it will come down almost vertically. Other golfers prefer a lower trajectory, even when playing downwind. However, when Jack and other top golfers play into wind, they want to reduce backspin. They do this, more often than not, by swinging easier with a longer club.

Crosswinds can be accommodated by fading the ball into a wind coming from the right and by drawing it into a wind coming from the left. These techniques are used by the pros, although the average golfer who cannot fade or draw at will is better off hitting the ball to the left or right as best he can and allowing the wind to bring it back on line. Higher handicappers might try to ease up on their swing, which will tend to reduce backspin and keep the ball low. Gary Player, an excellent wind player, recommends overclubbing by two clubs – choosing a five iron instead of a seven, for example – and trying to hit the ball the same distance you would with the shorter club. Knowing how to keep the ball down is important when playing in wind. And, to play the Old Course effectively, you must learn to play the wind.

9
END
356 YARDS · PAR 4

*Looking toward the ninth green, in the foreground.
This is the easiest hole on the course. Stretching out
beyond the green are the New and the Jubilee.*

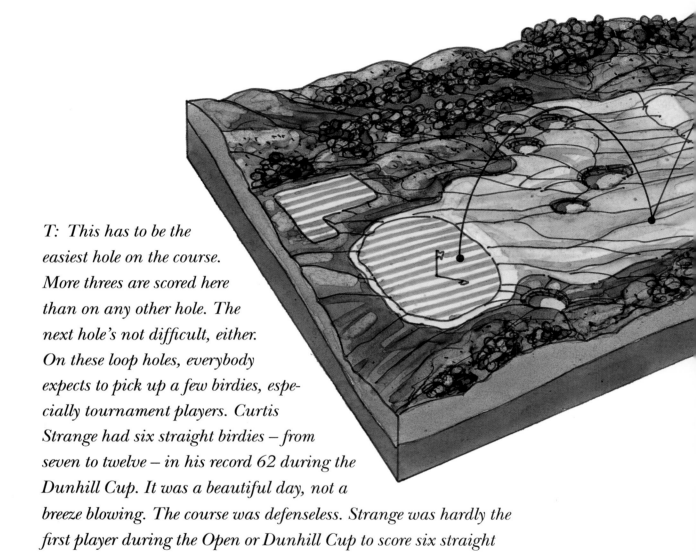

T: This has to be the easiest hole on the course. More threes are scored here than on any other hole. The next hole's not difficult, either. On these loop holes, everybody expects to pick up a few birdies, especially tournament players. Curtis Strange had six straight birdies – from seven to twelve – in his record 62 during the Dunhill Cup. It was a beautiful day, not a breeze blowing. The course was defenseless. Strange was hardly the first player during the Open or Dunhill Cup to score six straight birdies there, but then he managed four more for the rest of his round.

D: I know that John Daly drives this green regularly, but in today's conditions, most good players could, too.

T: Many of them have. Tony Jacklin eagled it in 1970 when he was out in 29. He should have gone over the green with his second, but it hit the pin and the ball dropped straight in the hole. All ye really have to worry about

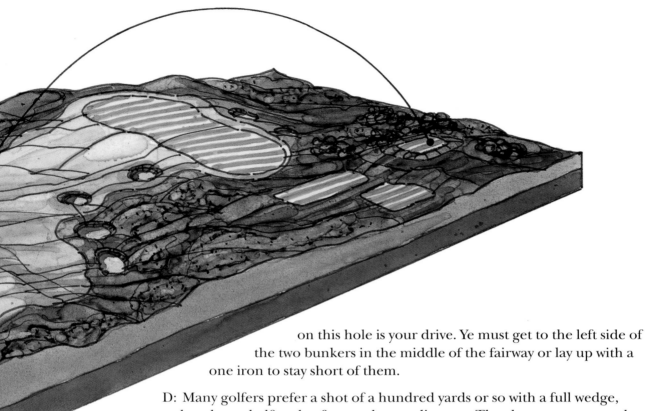

on this hole is your drive. Ye must get to the left side of the two bunkers in the middle of the fairway or lay up with a one iron to stay short of them.

D: Many golfers prefer a shot of a hundred yards or so with a full wedge, rather than a half-wedge from a shorter distance. They have more control.

T: That's quite true.

D: Do these bunkers have names?

T: Aye, they're called Boase Bunkers. They're named after a former provost of St. Andrews. I live on Boase Street.

D: I was always fascinated by the bunkers called Mr. and Mrs. Kruger and wondered where they came from. Apparently, they were Boers – Dutch South Africans. Mr. Kruger was president of the Transvaal during the so-called Boer War, which lasted from 1899 to 1902. Freddie Tait, the great English player, was killed in that war. According to legend, the Krugers were a thoroughly unpleasant, treacherous couple, so naturally the bunkers were named for them. I understand they were added to the Old Course in the early twentieth century, part of the epidemic of new bunkers built to curb the extra length of the Haskell ball. You might have thought they'd have put these bunkers more in play, though.

T: They're no longer treacherous. They're out of play. Mr. Kruger is eighty yards from the tee, and Mrs. Kruger about one hundred fifty.

D: That tough old couple must be turning in their graves. Yesterday, I told our photographer friend, Brian Morgan, they were out of play and, straightaway, he skied his drive and it went the full eighty yards directly into Mr.

Kruger. This bunker can also come into play if you push your drive on the tenth. Considering the wind and the capriciousness of the game, none of the bunkers on the Old Course is totally out of play.

T: This hole fools people; they misjudge the distance of their pitch. Because there are no bunkers at the green to reference the shot, good players tend to get careless; otherwise, it's quite easy.

D: These wide-open holes make the course much more fun for the average golfer, as do the short carries – as long as there is no wind. Even for the low handicappers, I think a hole like this has a place on a golf course, if only to help assess the quality of the other holes. As a former surfer, I know that if you don't have any troughs, you can't have any crests. Number nine is a relief after all those difficult, blind tee shots and plateau'd greens. Holes like this allow you to take a deep breath before you plunge toward home. As soon as we turn back toward the town, I always feel colder for some reason. Maybe it's the wind direction.

The ninth tee. Hit to the left to avoid the bunkers.

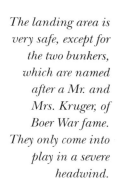

The landing area is very safe, except for the two bunkers, which are named after a Mr. and Mrs. Kruger, of Boer War fame. They only come into play in a severe headwind.

T: Perhaps because ye're used to a warmer climate. D'ye know that eight out of ten golfers without a caddie leave their approach short on nine?

D: That's because there's no clear orientation point near the bunker to help a player judge the distance from the landing area. Architecturally, the green, like many on the Old Course, presents a thin wafer as a target so you can't see how far its surface extends. The big, flat green merges imperceptibly into the wide, flat fairway. In this way, the entire green practically disappears. It's another illusion, like at number five – a vanishing trick. Even if you know the correct distance, it's still difficult to sense how far away from

THE LANDSCAPE AND SURROUNDS

Once the Old Course was a sandy waste, reclaimed from the sea and rather remote from the town. Today, it is impossible to divorce the Old Course from buildings. I've discussed the more recent additions elsewhere, but it's no secret that I find the new museum, hotel, clubhouse, and driving range inappropriate, even distasteful. As the sole owner of a firm of golf course architects, and a planner and designer of urban and golf course communities, I'm involved with the relationship between buildings and golf courses on an almost daily basis. No golf course is more intimately associated with a town than St. Andrews. On the first tee, you are aware of the consistent urban form of the old town itself, including the continuous flank of three-story town houses alongside the golf course – Rusack's Hotel, the St. Andrews Club, the University Building, the r&a Clubhouse. These friendly if rather austere buildings seem to greet, welcome, and hold the first and eighteenth holes in a rectangular embrace. They provide a defined space, an outdoor room and stadium for the start and finish of a tournament.

the hole you are, and such mental conflicts are part of the game. You tell me, Tip, that it's seventy-five yards from those bunkers, but if I didn't know that, I'd just as easily guess it was forty-five or fifty.

T: It's a very big green, and has some slopes with borrow.

D: This green is gigantic, about two-thirds of an acre. It's a single green, but half the size of the double-green at Hole O'Cross; I'd say close to thirty thousand square feet. That's probably the world's biggest single green. No green is completely flat, and this one has a few variations of slope and thin rolls that take character to read. I'm amazed how the wind blows the putts off line on this course. Putts of twenty feet can be blown several feet off the intended line, and short putts several inches. The wind picks up over the flat fairway just as it does over a lake, so the green is particularly vulnerable to wind. On the left side of the green is a small, deep bunker and heavy gorse tight against the green. If the wind's across the fairway, you've got a tough pin position there.

T: Ye have, indeed.

D: There are many stories about this hole, but the best, I think, is of Jock Hutchison, who was in the process of winning the Open in 1921.

T: Aye, he had just scored a hole in one on number eight. The ground was hard, and his drive on the ninth was skipping along toward the hole when a player in front ran out and removed the flag. The ball went into the hole and only just dribbled out again. The two successive holes in one would have been a tournament record.

AT THE TURN

The second hole is dominated by the Old Course Hotel, whose awkward facade rises above and beyond the parallel seventeenth. On the third hole, the course leaves the hotel behind much like a boat making for the open sea, and on the fourth tee, the countryside and distant hills beckon. Then, halfway through number four, suddenly the town is left behind. In just a few yards, the bounds of brick and mortar are cast off and you move into a more open landscape. There is a mounting sense of relief to be away from conflict and congestion, surely what is most precious about golf. The bracing freshness of the Eden estuary is felt, along with a slight chill from the North Sea. It is a world of steel grays, pale greens, and soft ochres, of sea smells and aromas of turf and heather, and of bird cries that almost hurt the ears. From this point onward, the woodland and hills are sharply defined before you.

At number six, water is seen for the first time and the far shore across Eden becomes clearer as you draw nearer. The view back from the sixth green blends town and countryside with vertical accents from the church towers, like Siena seen from the hills of Tuscany. Today, with a fresh breeze coming off the sea and the distant hills, you can almost feel the spirit of the Highlands and its peoples. On the seventh tee, you leave gorse behind, and on number eight, a new panorama emerges toward the town dominated by low, silhouetted hills. As you walk toward the town, there is a sense that the buildings come out to enfold and protect you, even there on the edge of the windswept peninsula. Holes nine and ten give off a liberating feeling of space. The double fairway is bracketed by gorse on two sides, with the distant town on one end and water on the other. The wide, flat savannah is an echo of the meadow on numbers one and eighteen, the end of one nine and the beginning of another. Together, these broad havens provide anchors for the course, a moderating balance to the high rough and heavy gorse that both proceeds and follows them. One seldom hears the landscape of the Old Course described in detail, but without these characteristic features, it would not and could not be what it is.

10

BOBBY JONES
318 YARDS · PAR 4

*Many golfers can drive the green here,
if the wind is favourable*

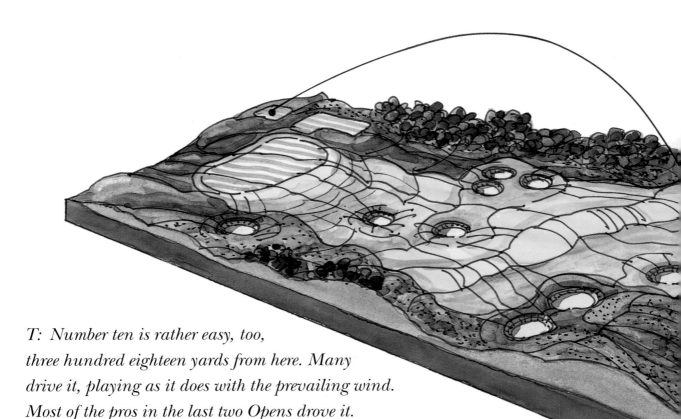

T: Number ten is rather easy, too,
three hundred eighteen yards from here. Many
drive it, playing as it does with the prevailing wind.
Most of the pros in the last two Opens drove it.

D: These fairways at nine and ten resemble those at one and eighteen – they're just as flat and wide, but are way out here by the Eden at the far end of the course. You might say that the Old Course is stabilized by these two double fairways at either end. This one here sort of dissolves into the flatness of the sea. The tenth green is joined to number eight, but is plateau'd at the front.

T: Aye, it also has some severe rolls and slopes away a bit to the left. The fairway bunker out there on the right really does come into play on this hole. It's two hundred fifty yards from the back of the tee to the front of the bunker. Knowing the yardages from tee to trouble, and trouble to green, helps here, of course. The bunkers on this hole catch a lot of tee shots, and they're a definite penalty.

D: It's a funny hole. Four handsome bunkers on the left are out of play – except for the reverse course.

T: Ye want to hit the ball down the middle, but ye must leave it slightly to the right.

D: There's a small, abrupt mound in the center of the fairway that seems out of place, while an adjacent bunker acts like a magnet for gathering balls that land nearby – just as the Road Bunker does at seventeen.

T: They sometimes take a one or two iron off that tee if the bunker is reachable, and the green is na'. But on the approach, nae half measures. Ye have to go to the extreme.

D: What do you mean, Tip?

T: Because of the roll of the slope in front of the green, which is inclined toward ye, ye may have to hit a five or six iron. Ye can hit it low through the rolling ground, but ye must na' try to hit a pitch through the air that'll be *half in* the air and *half down*. There's no half measure on this hole. Ye could hit a sand wedge high in the air and stop it on the green, but if ye're going to hit a pitch and run, ye'll have to roll it most of the way because some of the green slopes away from ye, and there's a step down toward the back. The professionals don't like the pitch and run because of the lottery of going over the bumps and mounds. If they do try a pitch and run, it would most likely be done with a seven iron.

D: I've seen Walter Woods and some of the other locals play some amazing running shots on this hole, and on number twelve. Walter hit one yesterday about sixty yards down a dip and over the mounds, then down and away again onto the green, stopping about ten feet from the pin. How often, Tip, would you say the pros hit a pitch and run at St. Andrews?

T: Na' very often. As little as possible, maybe two or three times a round; they prefer to have more control.

D: It depends on the wind. I suppose that European pros use it more, though, because they're used to pitching and running to hard greens.

T: I know Lema used it about three times per round. If ye grow up playing on links courses, ye learn to use your imagination more.

D: A couple of holes at the Augusta National were modeled after St. Andrews for their pitch and run characteristics – the fifth, the eighth, and the fourteenth, for example – but Augusta doesn't get much wind during the tournament. Also, the club tends to overwater the approaches, so the ball doesn't run much. You must have the same problem now that you are irrigating the Old Course.

T: Aye, it's a different golf course since they started irrigating, but we had to do it because of the great increase in play over the last thirty years. But due to the wind, it's still much harder and drier than an inland golf course.

D: If you go left here, you're in the heather. As you say, Tip, heather is nice to look at, but hard on your wrists. There's a bank of tired-looking heather over there on the left.

T: Once heather covered the entire fairway on this hole, and on number nine. Old Tom Morris cut both these fairways out of the heather.

D: In America, they complain about too much water. Heather's tough and wiry, but is still green vegetation and can stand only so much abuse from foot traffic. The groups of whins around this hole are particularly handsome. You can see an occasional white beam, that small tree with silvery leaves. It seems to be colonizing the course.

T: I know they are just here, but ye don't notice trees much on the Old Course. I think they take them out if they get too big.

D: The heather is growing on some pretty severe rolls, and the fairway seems to narrow the farther you get away from the tee. I see some really nasty lies.

The bunkers on the right catch many misplaced tee shots.

If your drive goes left, your're in the heather.

The bunkers to the right are deep, maybe six feet, with turf walls that have foreign grasses and other weeds growing from them. I've noticed on this hole that some pros lay up so they can get a full nine iron to the green. To my eye, the ninth green has a strange, alien quality. You can get lost in its flatness and lack of definition. But the green on this tenth hole, in spite of its stepped slope, seems forgiving and welcoming. It's a very friendly green.

NAMED FOR BOBBY JONES

The hole is named for Robert Tyre Jones Jr., the immortal Bobby who captured thirteen major titles in eight years, including the Grand Slam in 1930. No one has approached his record, and no one will. He won the United States Open in 1923, 1926, 1929, and 1930, was beaten in playoffs for two others, in 1925 and 1928, and finished second in 1922 and 1924. He took the American Amateur crown in 1924, and repeated it in 1925, 1927, 1928, and 1930; he finished second in this event in 1919 and 1926. Besides winning the two American championships in 1930, Bobby won the British Open and Amateur championships, then retired at the age of twenty-eight. During the time he was playing competitive golf, Jones obtained degrees in mechanical engineering from Georgia Tech and English literature from Harvard. After studying law for only one year at Emory University, he passed the Georgia bar in 1928, and began practicing law. He was a true amateur. He played golf for three months a year, no more. In 1928 and 1929, he competed each year in only five tournaments. Great professional players of the period, such as Walter Hagen and Gene Sarazen, seldom beat him. In 1930, Jones played in eight tournaments, including the Walker Cup matches.

Jones hated the Old Course when he first played it in 1921. After making the turn in forty-three and taking six at the tenth hole, Bobby drove into Hill Bunker at eleven, and left it there. He picked up in disgust, although he played out his round. In 1927, however, he returned to the Old Course and won the Open. He said it took thirteen rounds to discover the subtleties of the course. In the end, he came to love the Old Course above all others. In 1958, as every golfer in the world knows, Bobby Jones was given the freedom of the Burgh of St. Andrews, the only golfer and the only American other than Benjamin Franklin to receive this honor. In his book A Farewell to Sport, Paul Gallico, a leading sportswriter of the twenties and thirties, said of Jones: "I have found only one figure in sports who could stand up in every way as a gentleman as well as a celebrity; a fine, decent, human being as well as a newsprint personage, and one who never once

HIGH IN

176 YARDS · PAR 3

A dramatic par three of world renown. On a still day, the pros would
hit a seven iron, but in the wind, they would need anything from a
driver to a nine iron. The seventh flag is on the left.

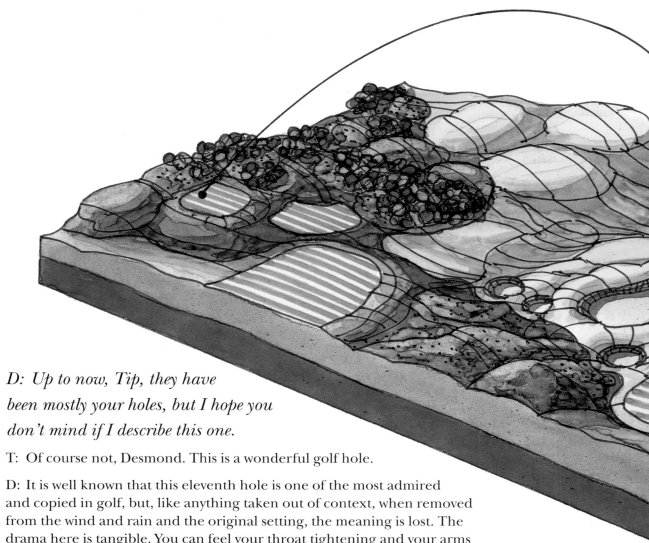

D: Up to now, Tip, they have been mostly your holes, but I hope you don't mind if I describe this one.

T: Of course not, Desmond. This is a wonderful golf hole.

D: It is well known that this eleventh hole is one of the most admired and copied in golf, but, like anything taken out of context, when removed from the wind and rain and the original setting, the meaning is lost. The drama here is tangible. You can feel your throat tightening and your arms stiffening just walking towards the tee. What a tough shot ahead, with those brooding ramparts of Hill and Strath to carry. Then, as a final test of nerve, the steep slope on the putting surface above. The cluster of higher tees must have been built quite recently, Tip, but I'm sure you don't like them.

T: No, it's a better hole from down here.

D: You may be right. You can certainly see a lot more of the green from up there, but the shot from this lower tee is more challenging. Up there, you can see the water, which adds a dramatic quality even if it's not in play. But what a view there is from the higher tee with the light green trees across the estuary and the lavender hills beyond! The Strath and Hill bunkers are perfect; they cut into the green at exactly the right points relative to the slopes. When you look at one, the other is always at the edge of your mind, flickering in your peripheral vision and forcing you to consider then reconsider the direction of your shot. And then, there's Cockleshell in the other corner of your eye, the archetypal visual bunker. Even if out of play, it's enough to put the fear of the Almighty into anyone. Just by its presence, Cockleshell focuses the power and energy of Strath and Hill. I always think these three bunkers, taken together, are a definition of the true nature of golf hazards.

T: The line of your tee shot is on that pillar, which is miles away at the Royal Air Force Station in Leuchars across the water, where occasionally a Concorde has landed bringing players from America to the Open. On a beautiful day like this, the professionals would play a seven iron off the tee, but with the changing wind, it can be anything from a full wood to a nine iron.

D: The wind can blow from any direction off the Eden, so your choice of club has to vary with the day. The view from the upper tee is overwhelming in all directions, but the green is the hub. I'm sure the wind is much stronger up here, although you would hardly notice it today. The plateau of the green seems much more ominous from the lower tee because it's partly hidden, but from the tee above, the bunkers are agonizing and the sheet of water is high drama. *(Climbing)* From up here, you have the sense you can almost stretch out and touch Strath and Hill and Cockle – porcelain teacups, with the water beyond shining like a giant silver tray.

T: At one time, this high tee was a spectator mound, and all the onlookers used to sit up here.

D: This must have been the father of spectator mounds. You can see several holes from this vantage. You can see, too, the vicious slope on the green, which can't be seen from the lower tee.

T: It was two consecutive days like this, dead flat calm, when Roger Davis, the Australian, had a 63 one day, and Curtis Strange a 62 the next. Very unusual weather, even though the Dunhill Cup is held in October.

D: Hill Bunker deserves to be called a trap. How deep is it?

T: Ten feet. Cockleshell is pretty deep, too, but it's hard to keep sand in it when there's wind.

D: This green may have the steepest continuous slope in the world, but at least it's one that slopes toward you and from above, at least, presents a clearly visible target, unlike most of the greens at St. Andrews. That's an advantage, but it makes this hole the most open to the elements.

T: It makes the green surface dry and very fast. Ye want to have an uphill putt on this hole. Unless the grass is grown long, a downhill putt won't stop, and sidehill putts have a borrow ye won't believe.

D: I'll believe anything about this hole, Tip. You can't take your eyes off any of the bunkers, but for all the sheer mass of Cockle, Strath is easily the most dominant. Yesterday, I saw a fellow hit into Strath, and in attempting to escape, hit the turf wall five times before turning around and playing out backwards. The poor fellow hit the other wall twice more, and eventually scored a twelve; I had to pretend I wasn't watching. Strath is undoubtedly the most significant greenside bunker anywhere. Hill Bunker is like a bottomless, circular well with those dark, gloomy shadows and invisible sand. I sometimes think Hill simply bores into the center of the earth. I've seen a few magical escape shots in the last two Opens, but players usually have to play the ball out backwards.

On a clear day, this is a glorious golf hole
that rewards a perfect tee shot.

A treacherously sloping green to putt. Downhill putts won't stop and sidehill putts have a tremendous borrow.

T: Then, if ye go over the green, ye're in deep trouble. There's the Eden River, deep rough, and that little bunker Bobby Jones got in once right at the back of the hole.

D: Back to front, there's probably a ten percent downhill slope on this green; I doubt that anyone could stop the ball on this fast, dry surface. The slope bottoms out and then comes up again at the lip of Strath Bunker like the cross section of a wave. There's an enormous tension between the steep slope of the green and the menace of Strath, and this is transmitted to the golfer. You want to land the ball just over the bunker's lip and stop it in the hollow to avoid the slope and the nasty, downhill putt, but that's the problem. In a tournament, you'd have to be desperate to go for the pin when it's behind Strath. The sensible shot is to the right of Strath, and hope for a reasonable line to the hole.

T: Ye'll find it's no' so easy to get putts close from the right side, owing to the wind. Ye're likely to leave most putts in the six-to-ten-foot range.

D: In the 1990 Open, Fred Couples hit into Strath, took two to get out, but holed the next for a four. Not every adventure here is a disaster. In the 1995 Open, I saw one player come out of Strath to the top of the green, then sink a long, curling, downhill putt that surely would have curled back into Strath if it hadn't gone in. In the third round, Nick Faldo was having troubles, which seemed to deepen when a strong wind blew his tee shot into Strath. In front of a groaning home crowd, he lofted his bunker shot almost vertically, and it slid down the flagstaff into the cup.

ON THE IDEAL HOLE

The eleventh hole is the inspiration for the fourth hole at Augusta National Golf Club. The fourth green at Augusta is not as steep as the original, but it is as fast and is now played fifty yards longer than originally designed. Alister Mackenzie, the codesigner of Augusta National, wrote the following in the June 1932 issue of *American Golfer*: "The Eden hole on the Old Course at St. Andrews, Scotland, owes its reputation almost entirely to the superlative excellence of its golfing features. It has a large green, sixty yards wide, but the slopes have such a character that it requires a greater variety of shots and gives rise to more thrills and excitement than any other hole. The various copies that have been made of this hole lack the severe slopes of the original and, comparatively speaking, are dull and insipid."

In a discussion of the best golf holes published in the October 16, 1906, issue of the British magazine *Golf Illustrated*, several players refused to consider the Eden among the best holes because it was possible to putt the ball off the tee. Mackenzie's rejoinder three decades later: "Objections have been raised to the Eden hole, that it can be played with a putter, and this is true, although I have never seen anyone reaching the green with less than two putts. On the other hand, the writer is firmly convinced that no hole is ideal unless it can be played with a putter; an ideal hole should be pleasurable for everyone, and there are many elderly players and women and children who cannot drive further than an expert player armed with a putter."

HEATHERY IN

316 YARDS · PAR 4

*Another short par four with a wide fairway leading to the pin on
the left. This hole is less benign than it looks, however.*

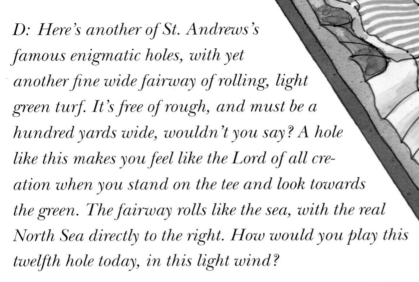

D: Here's another of St. Andrews's famous enigmatic holes, with yet another fine wide fairway of rolling, light green turf. It's free of rough, and must be a hundred yards wide, wouldn't you say? A hole like this makes you feel like the Lord of all creation when you stand on the tee and look towards the green. The fairway rolls like the sea, with the real North Sea directly to the right. How would you play this twelfth hole today, in this light wind?

T: At the moment, it's almost dead calm, so the pros would fly over all the trouble. On a day like this, or downwind, they'd mostly take a driver and try to drive the green. Anyway, they'd aim straight at the red flag. But into the wind, it's a long iron from the tee, and ye must place it carefully.

D: The green doesn't look very far away, and the fairway looks quite harmless and free of bunkers, even though we know they're out there waiting for us.

T: They're out there, all right, but ye can't see them. They're blind and dangerous. Ye've three hundred sixteen yards to carry everything to the flag, and two hundred twenty to carry the bunkers. Ye can drive this hole if the wind is right. When the winds was against, I gave Arnold a two iron and told him to hit away to the right. That took him just over two hundred yards, toward that large yellow bush, and kept him away from the bunker. From there, he'd have a pitch of one hundred ten yards to the pin.

D: Again, this is perceived as one of the easier holes here. Mind you, the blind bunkers lay a heavy psychological hand on the golfer.

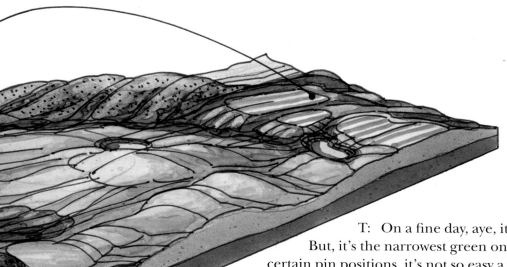

T: On a fine day, aye, it can be an easy hole. But, it's the narrowest green on the course and with certain pin positions, it's not so easy a target. Oddly enough, it's one of Jack Nicklaus's favorite golf holes.

D: Maybe he likes it because he rarely makes worse than three here. One has many reasons for choosing a favorite hole. I think Jack's really fond of short par fours, especially those with narrow, flat, exacting greens – like the fourteenth at Muirfield Village, Ohio. You must be very precise on a hole like this, but when you're naturally hitting them high, as Jack does, and bombing them in with his accuracy, even small targets seem bigger. Of course, he can also play a pitch and run when he wants to, and he's driven this green many times.

T: Arnold used to get birdies here, but the last two or three times he's played it, he's overclubbed. Each time, he took driver and knocked it over the bunkers, but he has na' made four yet.

D: Why?

T: He misjudged the pitch and run. Once, he pitched it right over the back, then knocked it up the hill and it came back down again. He took three to get down. That large bunker is Admiral's Bunker, named for Admiral Benson because he fell in while looking at a young lass. He was only eighty-six at the time.

D: What happened?

T: He used to carry his clubs – only six or seven, as I recall – and he's walking along and sees this beautiful blonde American girl in a red miniskirt and white shoes. She's already stopped traffic on several other holes, and she stops the old boy dead in his tracks. He turns round to keep his eye on her, takes a few steps backwards, and mutters to his partner, "I would na' mind posting a letter in *her* letterbox." Still walking backwards, he tumbles into the bunker, legs flailing wildly, turns a somersault, and lands on his head at the bottom. So they named the bunker for him.

D: Was he hurt?

T: No, I don't think so.

D: Was he a Scotsman?

T: No, an Englishman. He was a real character, a great old man.

D: This hole is famous for those five blind fairway bunkers. That makes it closer to a minefield than a golf hole. You need a navigator, not a caddie – an Admiral might do. They should rename it the Admiral's Hole.

T: Aye, this hole was definitely designed to be played the other way so that the bunkers can be seen from the reverse course.

D: Unfortunately, these bunkers are not much trouble for the pro, but they're bad news for the average player.

T: Into the wind, the good player can land between the bunkers with a long iron. Under all conditions, the average player has to hit it right. If he does, he'll have a nice easy shot to the pin. Nine times out of ten, I'll have him hit it short and right, leaving a seven or eight iron to the green. That's two clubs more than Arnold would need.

You can't really see the waiting bunkers from the tee, but they can be dangerous if there is a headwind.

Here you see what's patiently waiting for all ranks, even admirals.

D: There are four small bunkers three to six feet deep in the landing area, plus one like Mrs. Kruger – the Admiral's. There's a good level area of the fairway past the "invisible" bunkers, and your second here, though exacting enough to play, is a visible and pleasant contrast with the hidden peril of the tee shot. War and peace again; yin and yang. This contrast continues throughout the Old Course.

T: Ye need to carry the ball to this landing area; it's about two hundred seventy yards, but much less from the forward tee, and na' so bad if the wind's off the Eden.

D: There's a rewarding view of the green from this spot, but the small bunker in front catches quite a lot of the pros' drives. This is another handsome prospect approaching the green here. I like the way the land rolls and the way the bunkers are carved into the rolls like a Noguchi Garden. I always remember this hole because of the narrow ridge running right across the thin sliver of green. The surface appears to be sloping away from you, but that's an illusion. The ridge certainly gives you a frame, of sorts.

T: The green's not sloping away much; it's pretty flat. If ye're going anywhere, it's better that ye go over the green because it's easier to putt back to the pin than it is to putt from short of it.

D: Walter Woods favors a run up with a seven or eight iron here rather than a pitch, which can easily bounce off the putting surface to the back. The upper part of the green can't be more than thirty feet wide, and that doesn't leave much room for the pin. *(Actually, it's about eleven paces, or thirty-two feet across.)* I think this is another of St. Andrews's great holes, with a good central idea for golf course architecture. That's probably another reason

Jack likes it. Still, the hole is so obviously designed to be played from the opposite direction. The tee shot is really much more interesting if the hole's played backwards. But then, some holes on the reverse course had to be better than the regular course, if only to satisfy the law of averages.

T: That seems likely.

D: In 1990, Nick Faldo landed in the whins, chipped out, and got a four. In 1995, on the second day, I watched as Mark McCumber got in that little bunker just before the green. He had an impossible lie, inches from the wall. But he hooked it out high over his head, muttering to himself, and helanded on the green approximately one hundred fifty feet left of the pin. He two-putted for his par, the act of another true professional. On the last day, John Daly drove the green with his one iron and laid an eighty-foot putt almost stone dead for a three.

T: I always thought that Daly, with his long, accurate drives and good short game, would do well on the Old Course.

WEATHER AND FAIRWAYS

When I was growing up in England, there was no irrigation on our golf courses. When we played links courses, the most useful and most popular shot was the run up, the bump and run, or the pitch and run, as it is variously described. In those days, you looked for a sandy site before you built a golf course, so all the greens and fairways were made of sand. They were bone hard and dried out by the wind, which made them very firm, indeed. This same wind, which can deflect a ball much more suddenly and unpredictably than the most irregular slope, is both the reason for and the source of the run-up shot.

When the installation of irrigation systems was introduced in America, major companies like Rainbird and Toro made deserts bloom, spreading the idea worldwide. Consequently, irrigation greatly increased play on many golf courses, especially those that had little rain or where the rainfall was adequate, but inconsistent. These well-watered greens almost eliminated the pitch and run, reducing many places to target golf; the atmospheric feel of the game was almost gone. But the windy linksland courses in Britain still require playing a variety of different shots. Because of the wind and the sand-based greens, there are places where you cannot stop the pitched ball no matter how much backspin you put on it. Even on the well-irrigated courses in America, there are times when you try the pitch and run. For instance, when the green slopes away from you and the pin is at the back, you cannot stop the ball with a high pitch, and only the running shot will do. In spite of modern irrigation, St. Andrews with its wind and hard, flat greens is still often a pitch-and-run course. This shot requires a great deal more intelligence, intuition, and creativity than the ordinary lofted nine iron from a grooved swing. Because of weather conditions, the game of golf in Britain is more demanding, more subtle, more unpredictable, and ultimately more fulfilling than the American game. So you're not likely to hear a Scotsman groan, "If only the weather were better...."

HOLE O'CROSS IN

425 YARDS · PAR 4

*Looking toward the thirteenth green, the pin is at the
front of this double green. Altogether, a formidable hole
and one of the most difficult on the course.*

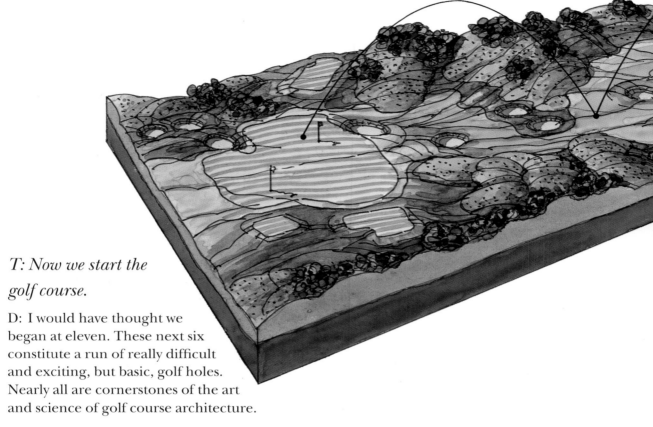

T: Now we start the golf course.

D: I would have thought we began at eleven. These next six constitute a run of really difficult and exciting, but basic, golf holes. Nearly all are cornerstones of the art and science of golf course architecture.

T: This thirteenth is one of the hardest holes, and ye can play it two ways, depending on where the pin is on the green. Today, the pin is in the middle, so ye can hit it up the right side, short of the dividing ridge of rough and anywhere on the fairway between the bunkers and the gorse. When the pin is on the right side of the green, over by the bunker, I'll tell the golfer to play left, over the Coffin Bunkers and onto the sixth fairway, where he'll have a good view of the green eight times out of ten. If ye go too far left, ye'll end up in the light rough with a blind shot, although the line is still good.

D: Is this another hole we owe to the reverse course?

T: Partly.

D: There are two distinct enclosed valleys on this hole, separated with the ridge of rough that stops most tee shots. In the Opens that I have watched, most professional players drive left, across Coffins, to the sixth fairway, just as you say, to get a look at the green.

T: Ye can see there is a large area for pin positions. If the hole is more than ten yards from the front of the green, ye'll have a straightforward shot. On a normal day with a breeze coming from the west, the tournament player and the amateur will play similar second shots.

D: I know this hole is very controversial because the narrow fairway returns to the other side of the Hole O'Cross green, at number five. With narrow fairways like this, the wind and weather must be crucial.

T: The prevailing wind on the golf courses here is westerly, but the weather at St. Andrews tends to be changeable. All the rains come from the west. The weather is usually settled and nice when the wind is easterly, yet the greenkeepers dread east winds because they dry out the greens, especially in the spring. East winds also tend to be cooler. It's no' uncommon at St. Andrews for the wind to change with the tide, and it's no' unusual to play the front nine against the west wind and the back nine against the east wind, a condition that also happens sometimes at Troon. That's where Palmer won the Open, and I caddied. He won it on the Railroad Hole in the most terrible weather. In his four rounds, he had one par, two birdies, and an eagle on that hole – even threes for four rounds, while everyone else was taking sevens and eights, and Nicklaus a ten.

D: You can't hit the ball forward if you're against the face of these bunkers unless you're a trick-shot artist like Seve, but like many of the holes on the Old Course, it's a much more reasonable test for the average golfer from the shorter tees. The hole is still challenging, but who's going to miss a green that's a hundred yards across with his second shot?

T: Ye'd be surprised.

D: Golf is a surprising game, but when they say you're hitting greens in regulation on this course, they're stretching things a bit. Out in the sixth fairway, left of the Coffins, there are some good lies, but there are mean-looking bunkers, Cats Trap and Walkenshaw, staring at you.

T: Those bunkers are about one hundred sixty yards from the green; most players would need a following wind to reach them from the tee.

D: There's not much chance of getting to the green if you're in them.

T: No.

D: It's ironic, but rather what you'd expect in the steady diet of contrast and ambiguity offered by this extraordinary golf course, and I imagine that this thirteenth is one of its more eccentric golf holes. It has the biggest green in the world, but you can't see it! If you want to have a look at the pin, you have to play to another fairway. That's the irony; surely, a golfer is better off playing his approach from over here in the sixth fairway where he can obtain a view of the green.

T: That's true, if he's good enough.

D: From the right side of the fairway, you can barely see the flag, but from over here on the left, you have a wide, handsome prospect over the second valley on this hole, revealing how all of its rolls and mounds and well-sculpted bunkers fit into the landscape. This was golf architect Tom Simpson's favorite golf hole, "the best in the world," he said.

T: It's a lot of people's favorite. I have never understood why this is stroke number twelve, and the ninth is stroke number five on the handicap index. The huge green, shared with the fifth, used to finish short of the present surface – Walter Woods built this peninsula extension seven or eight years ago.

D: The green has a fine rolling surface like a ruffled lake, perched up on a plateau that is almost a mesa and starts a hundred yards in front of the vast putting surface. The front addition must be at least eight thousand square feet in area, enough for a complete new green on most golf courses, and a large one at that. Most of the recent extensions at the Old Course are large.

This is the exact view of the green that a well-placed drive 250 yards out would have for the second shot.

More hazards surround the green to catch errant approach shots and bad bounces.

T: We need them because of the increase in play.

D: This area before the green is sure "whoopsy" – I mean, it rolls. You could almost put it in a fairground as a roller coaster. Tom Simpson liked the fact that the green sloped away from you, but they need to put the pin in the back right, past the bunker, to establish the true greatness of the hole.

T: That's where they put it in tournaments. That's what fixes the holes on the Old Course – where they put the pin in tournaments.

D: There are three good-sized rolls to negotiate on the right side.

T: Sometimes, ye'd want to play safe, just up the left.

D: This hole seemed to perplex Norman during his duel with Faldo in the 1990 Open. He bogeyed it the last two days. The green seemed to confuse him. You could easily add another hundred yards to this hole by changing the pin position, and then, there's the east or the west wind to contend with. With its new extra surface, the Hole O'Cross green is now longitudinal in shape and quite a bit wider than the fairway.

T: There's another nasty little bunker, too, that Walter has rebuilt for us.

D: Does it have a name?

T: No, they don't all have names.

D: Walter says there are only a hundred seventeen bunkers on the course. There seem to be more. Many have been filled in and are now grass bunkers, but they remain severe hazards – you can spot them all over the golf course.

AN AGELESS STRUCTURE AND CHARACTER

What Tom Simpson probably liked most about this hole was the clarity in the disposition of its structural elements. We've already described the powerful rhythmic grades and broken vegetation of the hills adjacent to the sixth tee, the collateral hole. These remind me of the land around Kathmandu in Nepal. Not only do the hills on the left come into play, as the fairways are almost interchangeable at this point, but they extend across the thirteenth fairway and end in an escarpment at the right, which blocks the view of the green from the tee. Ranging across these hills on the right hand is a persistently thick block of heather and gorse that runs up behind the fourteenth tee. To the left of the fairway, dividing it from the sixth and coming into play with most driving strategies, is a dotted line of bunkers starting with Nick's, which is quite close and seldom a problem, then the two huge ominous bunkers called Coffins at two hundred twenty to two hundred forty yards, and ending with Cats Trap and Walkenshaw at three hundred yards plus; these last are set with great flair into the diagonal escarpment.

Simpson was a bon vivant who drove a Rolls Royce, and an aesthete who went on holidays to the south of France. No doubt he found this hole, as I do, very beautiful, with the fundamental bone structure and form that seems ageless in some women, and in a few golf courses. Its underlying character and structure projects a radiance and mood that provides a winning theater for the game of golf. The aesthetics of the fairway shapes and bunkers are architectural. I feel quite certain that some were made, rather than found – the forms are too consistent to be otherwise. With such an original character, the thirteenth hole is the mother of Sunningdale, Pine Valley, and Cypress Point, which themselves are parents of many other golf courses around the world. They say that Scotland has no climate, only weather. If so, number thirteen is a hole for all golfers in all seasons, in all weather, and in all climactic conditions.

The walk between the whins from the thirteenth green to the fourteenth tee truly sings. We golf architects should put more effort into designing the walks between holes. I once conducted a survey of some seniors playing on a course I'd designed in Wheaton, Maryland, in the United States. It was a carefully composed golf course, and I thought they'd talk about the shotmaking. But none of them mentioned their tee shots, the drawn and faded approaches, or the angles and undulations of the putting surfaces. What they liked best and what they talked about were the shaded walks between the holes. There's no need for shade at St. Andrews, of course, but these little patches of natural environment are welcome respites, indeed.

LONG

567 YARDS · PAR 5

*From the fourteenth tee the drive must be aimed directly for the steeple in the
far distance. On the right is out-of-bounds; on the left are four bunkers.
Along with seventeen, the most difficult tee shot on the course.*

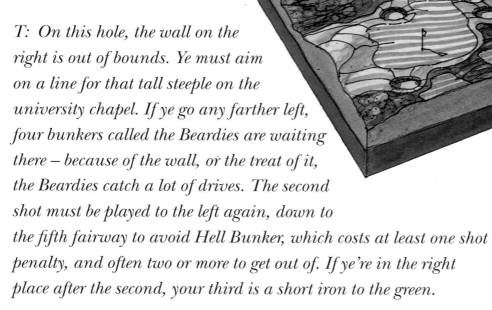

T: On this hole, the wall on the right is out of bounds. Ye must aim on a line for that tall steeple on the university chapel. If ye go any farther left, four bunkers called the Beardies are waiting there – because of the wall, or the treat of it, the Beardies catch a lot of drives. The second shot must be played to the left again, down to the fifth fairway to avoid Hell Bunker, which costs at least one shot penalty, and often two or more to get out of. If ye're in the right place after the second, your third is a short iron to the green.

D: I believe fourteen was Bobby Jones's favorite hole.

T: Aye, it's a good one.

D: I gather that Jones liked this hole because of the angle of the green, which is supposed to favor the golfer who plays from the left. But it's always seemed to me that the surface sloped away or at best was level when coming in from that side. I believe it's true that Jones liked to hit it past the green and play back to the hole up the more receptive slope. This is a tactic much like playing your second at the seventeenth to the left, near the Swilcan Burn Bridge, then pitching safely on, an old reverse course maneuver.

T: But ye must come in from the left. Ye've no shot from the right – well, at best, a very difficult one. To avoid Hell Bunker, your second shot must be away left, perhaps fifty yards.

Aim for the big red building to the right of the R and A Clubhouse. What a difficult drive this is, out of bounds on the right, the Beardies waiting on the left. Bill Rogers, the 1981 Open Champion, hit three balls out of bounds here in 1984, and took twelve! Nicklaus once drove out of bounds over the wall, hit another into the Beardies, took two to get out, and wrote down an eight. In the 1995 Open, Jack was in the Beardies again, and later took four to get out of Hell, which led to a very unusual ten on a hole that he has so often birdied, and even eagled, in the past.

D: Sarazen and many another household name have taken eights or more on this hole. The Beardies are vicious bunkers. I always picture them as six, yet I know there are only four. They point in all directions, another relic of the reverse course. Those bunkers must be at least fifty yards from the wall, but Jack Nicklaus swears they're only thirty; that's the measurement he used in building his replica of the Old Course in Orlando, Florida. I notice the wind has changed round as we've been talking and is now in our faces.

T: Aye. As I say, if the wind changes with the tide, some days ye can play into the wind all the way out and all the way back. The line is on the tallest spire ye can see, and the Beardies are over there on the left, so it's a very narrow line.

D: How long must you hit your drive to carry the angle of the wall?

T: The wall is just over two hundred yards from the back tee, so ye should hit it at least two hundred twenty, maybe two hundred thirty yards.

D: Is this the toughest tee shot on the course?

T: This, and number seventeen.

D: What a splendid combination of grass grades and plant forms there are in front of the tee. I really like the way you go down here and see lusty hassocks of grass all around these wavelike rools covered with cyprus reeds. There's peat, as well; this is really old St. Andrews.

T: It's been like that since I can remember.

D: This small area captures the genuine character of links golf, one that everyone seems willing to spend millions to build and maintain on the new

*The fourteenth fairway is on the left, and we are looking
back to the tee from the green in the foreground.*

Hell Bunker, which must be avoided at all costs. Its immense scale is shown by the two figures of Desmond and Tip.

American Scottish-style courses. Sadly, these courses seldom come close to the spirit that's present at St. Andrews. But then, what course could? I doubt there's another golf course in the world that has the presence, the character, and environmental rightness of this one.

T: Ye're right, Des. They all agree. Even Gary Player says that. Although the New Course is a good one, too.

D: Yes, but it doesn't have the atmosphere, the sense of quality. The New Course suffers from lack of loving care and the reverential treatment the Old Course receives as its birthright.

T: The New Course has na' the character, no. The Old Course is a fine course, but it should be in better shape. They're playing too many rounds on it.

D: That's a major problem for the future. Every golfer in the world wants to play here, and to say he has.

T: Everybody *can't* play the Old Course. That's why they have the ballot.

D: I notice that some fellows pull their second shots too far and land in the heather on number five. That's a bad patch of heather, but they're trying to avoid the Beardies. Personally, I find them repellent bunkers, alien, sneaky, and underhanded, like little pit bulls lurking in the grass waiting to snap at unsuspecting golfers.

T: Nobody likes to get in the Beardies.

D: They're shallower than most. Walter Woods says they couldn't be much deeper because of the water table, but I remember them being deeper once.

This uneven rough awaits even well-placed second shots if they run through the fairway.

T: I believe they were, too. All the caddies reckon they were deeper years ago. The line for the tee shot is almost exactly the line for the second shot – aim to the left side of that same university chapel steeple.

D: Don't the Elysian Fields give us a broad, comforting piece of fairway? If you can hit a good tee shot, it's like landing in heaven. But then, it ought to – Elysium in Greek mythology was a place of ideal happiness. The turf is pliant and receptive. A drive to the lower level of the fairway on number five does take all the dangers – the wall, the Beardies, and Hell – out of play.

T: That's why I like it, but ye have to be careful no' to go too far, especially if the wind is strong. Ye must na' go over the fairway.

D: How would you club a professional, Tip?

T: Something like a two iron, I'd say. If he could knock it about two hundred sixty yards from the back tee, with little or no wind, he might try to carry everything; he could just go for it. From there, it would be two hundred sixty to two hundred eighty yards to the flag. Greg Norman, Davis Love, and this even longer man, John Daly, can make it on most days, depending on the wind.

D: That would have to be with a wood.

T: Yes, probably a three wood, but it would all depend on the wind, the player, and the amount of roll that day.

D: There's a fine, natural valley running up to the left of the green from this spot on the fifth fairway. To the right, you have a series of folds and a big grass bunker adjacent to the green that will gather balls bouncing in that direction. And then there's Hell. Is it true, Tip, that Arnold drove into Hell Bunker and said, "Tip, you didn't tell me that bunker was there," and that you replied, "No, Arnold, but you didn't tell me you were going to drive it three hundred ninety yards!"

T: Aye, it is.

D: The fourteenth is like a golf course unto itself, and Hell Bunker its icon, golf's most significantly placed bunker. The Old Course pivots around it. You start thinking about Hell on the fifth hole, when you first see it out of the corner of your eye. It comes into focus again as you approach the thirteenth green where it looms a short distance in front of you, making the putt on thirteen that much harder.

T: No one who has ever played the Old Course forgets the Hell Bunker.

D: Hell has a small valley of its own, and is many-sided. Obviously, it was fashioned originally for the reverse course. A few yards past, Tip, is your bunker, called the Kitchen Bunker, or Hell's Kitchen. I'm told that you holed out from there with a seven iron for an eagle three when you won the St. Andrews Boys Championship.

T: I had to hit it hard to get the ball out, and it bounced into the hole. It's one hundred forty yards to the front of the green.

D: I know Hell was deeper when I was growing up – fourteen to sixteen feet, perhaps. Maybe they cut down the top when they rebuilt it. I'm sure there's at least three feet of sand in the bottom.

T: That's quite possible.

D: What about Grave Bunker, the one beyond Hell, just nearer the green? These two have been around for a long time.

T: Nobody knows how long; as far as I can make out, they're prehistoric.

D: Another feature that interests me is the rough, scalloped ground to the right and in front of the hole. You don't hear it mentioned much, but you'd have a tough time getting out of that place. It looks more like the old St. Andrews.

T: That's what I'm saying, Desmond. Ye have to come in from the left.

D: I stood here and watched play during the 1990 Open and couldn't believe how many pros found the trouble on the right side with their second shots. Hard to believe they wouldn't have found this out in a practice round. What were their caddies doing? I noticed the same thing happening with the tee shots on sixteen and seventeen, too.

T: Some golfers do na' like to play on other fairways. Sometimes there's a crosswind.

D: The green slopes away from you, but why is the angle of approach so much better from the left? The surface, after all, still slopes away from the player, or so it seems.

T: Well, it's better because the undulations are on the other side; the ball can roll in and stay up on that level when ye come in from the left.

D: Yes, the green is flatter here, and it's easier to hold a shot from that side.

T: Ye have to come in from the left. Playing from the right, ye'd be in that bad ground and have almost no shot.

D: Augusta National is freely based on the Old Course, as we noted earlier. You should come to the States some time, Tip. It has some excellent courses, and I'm sure Arnold has tried to persuade you to go.

T: No' so much the last ten years, but the first ten he certainly did.

D: You might not recover if you did.

T: I've heard mixed opinions. People have told me, "Tip, you've done the right thing in staying where you are." All my family were here, the kids were young at the time, and that had something to do with it. But if there are many more people like Arnold in America, I know I would like the country.

THE EFFECTS OF TIME

The fourteenth is one of the seminal holes of golf. Its principles of multiple choice are widely used in golf architecture. You can play it a dozen different ways, depending on your game, but above all it requires insight and understanding. It is less visually dramatic than, perhaps, the eleventh hole, but like its sister, it's one you cannot forget. At Bobby Jones's suggestion, Alister Mackenzie tried to reproduce the idea of the fourteenth on number five at Augusta National, but it couldn't really work without the wind. All golf courses change in character, but people don't realize this because the change is gradual. A tee is altered one year, two traps and a green the next, then trees are planted, and in twenty years, you have a different golf course. Because of the lack of enlightened direction, most golf courses in the world are getting steadily worse, but, recently, the Old Course has been getting better. The complaints box in the R&A Clubhouse is a great help, but Walter Woods has improved the Old Course by his sense of rhythm and balance. He is responsible for the perfect line and mass of the whins. By all rights, he should be listed as an associate architect for the remodeling he has supervised. Nature is a collaborator, but not a designer; indeed, it's far down the list of designers of this golf course. Still, the work of man is such that the course seems natural, and this in itself is some sort of triumph. The truth is, the Old Course has been carefully manipulated with the same sort of refinement you might find in a Japanese garden. A lot of superintendents are changing golf courses every day, but very few do it well, and not one in a thousand as well as Walter Woods has done here.

15

CARTGATE IN

413 YARDS · PAR 4

*Looking back down the fifteenth fairway
from the green on the left.*

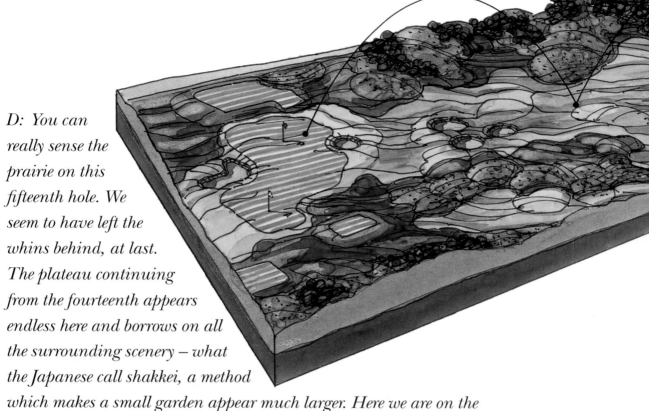

D: You can really sense the prairie on this fifteenth hole. We seem to have left the whins behind, at last. The plateau continuing from the fourteenth appears endless here and borrows on all the surrounding scenery – what the Japanese call shakkei, a method which makes a small garden appear much larger. Here we are on the back tee, Tip; they tell me it was made three feet higher a few years ago, and, as you know, I approve of that. This can be a very long par four, so you need a firm platform for your drive. The fairway is wide open; perhaps we need a breather after thirteen and fourteen. There may not be as much character to the golf on this hole as on the other holes of the inward half.

T: No, but the green on this hole is the most deceptive on the golf course. You will see what I mean when we are farther down this fairway.

D: Those two mounds on the right are kind of mesmeric. They're like big Henry Moore sculptures rising out of the flat prairie, drawing your eyes and holding them as you scan the fairway to assess its problems. They must be about two hundred fifty yards from the tee.

T: There are three bunkers way down there, though ye can only see two from here, at about three hundred thirty yards. They're called the Robs, and the line for the drive is straight toward the Robs.

D: Not many of my friends would be likely to get in them today.

T: Ye can reach them downwind, though. The out of bounds on the right is a concern, but the two clearly visible bunkers, the Robs, give ye the perfect line for the tee shot.

D: They look innocuous enough from the tee.

T: The Robs are definitely out of play today with this head wind, as I said. There is a flat area just behind the hill. Henry Cotton said this was the most deceptive hole on the course, and I think he was right. Most people underclub the second shot.

D: The green looks pretty close from the landing area.

T: If you hit a five to three iron from here, ye won't be far away. That bunker there, called Sutherland, is the one filled in by a green committee, then dug up again in the middle of the night. To his dying day, a man called Sutherland was blamed, yet actually it was two former captains of the club who dug the hole. It's a very small bunker and would na' have taken long to dig, would it? A nasty one, though – a little pot.

D: From the back tee, you'd get in the bunker only when there was a really stiff head wind, stronger than today.

T: Sutherland is two hundred thirty yards from the back tee, and one hundred eighty from the front of the green. As I say, it's a funny second shot because the green does na' look very big.

D: You need to hit the green with your second because there's broken ground with pronounced pockets and rolls in front of the green. The fairway is much narrower there. The green looks small because like most of the greens at St. Andrews, there doesn't seem to be much slope from back to front to help the golfer hold the shot. This green is mostly flat and even. Like the green on number nine, its surface joins to this flat fairway to present a compressed visual image, like a thin wafer. That's why it looks closer than it is. Illusion is part of the mystery and ambiguity found everywhere on this course.

T: Today, ye only need a six iron if approaching from this small valley between the mounds.

D: Maybe you'd choose an eight if you didn't know the illusion. Alister Mackenzie, a camouflage artist in World War I, liked this sort of effect. There is a typical St. Andrews dip in the green about twenty yards across, which is an example of why golfers tend to lose their sense of perspective in

*The second shot
needs to carry right
to the green to avoid
bad bounces and
the greenside
bunker.*

places. The three Robs and the swale in the fairway, stretching close to seventy yards from the last one to the green, provide another of the illusions that recur on the Old Course. Some people think Dick Wilson used that idea when he built bunkers about thirty yards from the very large greens at Arnold's golf course at Bay Hill in Florida. In actual fact, though, successive superintendents have marooned those front bunkers by reducing the size of the greens. This has happened on many other courses worldwide.

T: I've heard a lot about Bay Hill. Arnie talked about it all the time.

D: This fifteenth on the Old Course has a huge and beautiful green. I liked the adjoining green, number three, but the whole looks even better from over here. It's an essay in green design. I like the way the forms articulate the environment and the rolls continue out into the fairway. Two bunkers squeeze into the waist that joins with number three green. The small pot on the left is standard, but the Cartgate Bunker, which thrusts into the green and which we described earlier, is unique. Where would you aim, Tip?

T: Just to the left of the pin.

D: There are two humps at the right and back of the green. When the pin is back there, the hole plays close to four hundred fifty yards – and that would account for the consistent underclubbing.

T: Very few golfers go over the green. At the 1995 Open Championship, players were frequently caught out by the bunker behind the green because they were trying to get the ball up to the pin, but the balls kept rolling over the green. During the Open, the pin is more to the left than it is for normal play.

D: As Jack Nicklaus says, the key to this hole is distance, not direction. I've noticed that if you're playing into the prevailing west or southwest wind and you need a chip, pitch, or long putt, you may finish short of the hole because of the wind. Not only that, you'll find day-to-day variations due to the irregularities of the green's surface. Ernie Els took a five here in the third round in 1995 after driving the green. He was leading the tournament, but was never the same afterward. Four strokes after a long drive to an apparently flat, easy green can be quite unnerving.

T: Fifteen is the sort of hole that shakes you up a bit. It looks easy, but many fine golfers have taken five here when they expected three.

THE ILLUSION OF FAIRNESS

Many have extolled the risk-to-reward ratio on the Old Course, but you must have luck on your side when you play it. When Lema won his Open in 1964, he played his first two rounds in excellent morning weather. Nicklaus and other golfers playing in the afternoon were not so fortunate. They had gale winds and driving rain to contend with. Wind, weather, and lay of the land define linksland golf in Scotland, elements that are too often absent from the newly manufactured golf courses of Britain and America. Perhaps the more skillful golfers create their own breaks. Walter Travis said that luck is part of the game and a good golfer is good at all parts of it. Yet golf, like life, is hardly fair, and I doubt whether it was meant to be. A life without worries or problems is a sorry life, indeed. But, I would say that a great course has the *illusion* of fairness, and its conquerors borrow from it the illusion of invincibility. Great courses inspire the development of great players, a lesson still to be learned in many of the countries new to golf, for whom the Old Course provides an endless source of ideas and information.

To the amateur player, the fifteenth, like most of the holes on the inward half, is many holes in one. There are a number of choices on both the drive and the second shot, and if you play the hole well or make a small or large mistake, in each case you have to pull a commensurately effective recovery or strategic shot from your bag. The essence of good architecture is present here, which includes asking for a well-placed drive, shaped to the requirements of the hole and the conditions of weather, and the presentation of many variations of approaches, bunker shots, chips, and putts. On different days, in different winds, with different pin positions, a golfer might well use every club in the bag on this hole.

CORNER OF THE DYKE

382 YARDS · PAR 4

*Out-of-bounds is on the right, so play well left
and avoid the fairway bunkers as well.*

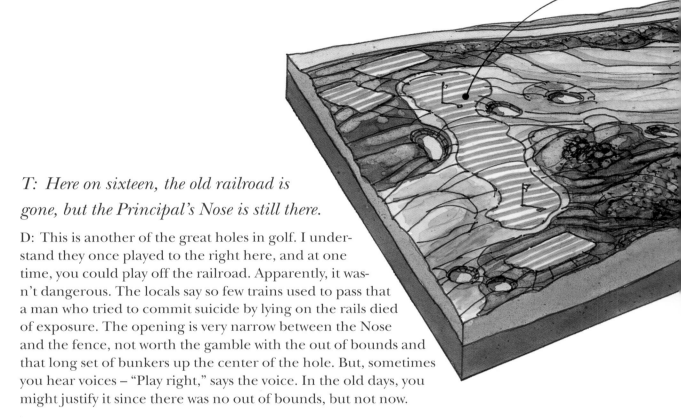

T: Here on sixteen, the old railroad is gone, but the Principal's Nose is still there.

D: This is another of the great holes in golf. I understand they once played to the right here, and at one time, you could play off the railroad. Apparently, it wasn't dangerous. The locals say so few trains used to pass that a man who tried to commit suicide by lying on the rails died of exposure. The opening is very narrow between the Nose and the fence, not worth the gamble with the out of bounds and that long set of bunkers up the center of the hole. But, sometimes you hear voices – "Play right," says the voice. In the old days, you might justify it since there was no out of bounds, but not now.

T: No, ye really must play left. When Arnold played his practice round for the Open in 1990, he drew the driver from his bag when we got to this tee. "That's wrong, sir, don't take a driver," I said. "There are bunkers waiting at the back of a straight drive, out of bounds on the right, with rough and heather on the left. So it's a two iron down the left side, then no more than a seven iron to the green." "So you tell me," Arnold said, a bit sarcastic; that's the way he talks to me. Then he turned to the crowd and said: "Are you listening to this guy here? Can you see what I've had to put up with for thirty years?" The crowd said, "Listen to him!" Arnold said, "Naw, gimme the driver," and he knocked it over the Principal's Nose but thirty yards left and into the rough. Gary Player, who was paired with us, said, "Tip, you've got it right," and hit a two iron to the perfect spot. Arnold grimaced and said, "Okay, Tip, you're right again."

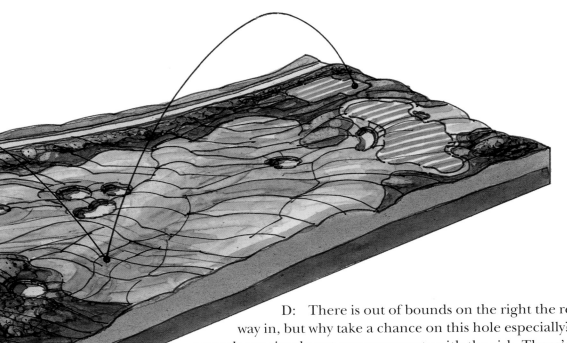

D: There is out of bounds on the right the rest of the way in, but why take a chance on this hole especially? The rewards are simply not commensurate with the risk. There's a fine piece of fairway out there on the left about two hundred to two hundred seventy-five yards. In the summer, it doesn't get dark until eleven o'clock, and on the holes close to the town the prudent golfer might take the opportunity to survey the ground the night before.

T: Would ye mind if I frown at that bit of advice?

D: You're quite right, excuse me. He'll listen to his caddie, won't he? Wasn't it Herb Wind who said if you don't take a caddie at St. Andrews, you deny yourself the wine of the country? Surely, you can hit a wood if you know where you're going on this hole, Tip. If the wind's coming from the right, you can aim the ball just out of bounds and let it float back again. That's one of the hairiest shots in golf, but didn't Kel Nagle play to the right just like that when he beat Arnie in the Centennial Open?

T: He did, but ye don't have to remind me of it. Just play left, it's the best way. Ye should play well left of the Wig Bunker, toward the right-hand steeple. Toward that little white house.

D: That's forty yards left, at least, maybe seventy yards left of the fence.

T: Aye, toward the Wee Kirk, Hope Park Kirk.

D: It has a handsome steeple, much nicer than the hotel's.

T: Maybe, but the hotel looks a lot better than it did. When they tore down Auchterlonie's Drying Sheds to build the hotel, they replaced the sheds with a net. As ye know, they built a copy of the sheds and restored the seventeenth fairway.

D: The area was once occupied by a railway depot complete with sidings, wasn't it, and didn't Auchterlonie take over one of the black sheds? British Rail was the original owners, and they built the Old Course Hotel after they took out the railroad.

T: That's right. If ye hit a one iron into this area near the Nose, ye'll have about a hundred fifty yards again. For the championship, they'll put the pin in between the two bunkers – Wig and the one guarding the front of the second hole. That's for the championship, mind you. Ye can see the shape of the green coming down the right side from the second shot, whereas, on this side, you've seventy to seventy-five yards and a difficult run up shot. So keep left.

The Principal's Nose Bunkers, which should be avoided by playing well left.

D: We're now about forty-five yards forward and to the side of the front bunker of the Principal's Nose.

T: Exactly. During the Dunhill Cup, if the green's receptive, the pros will hit an eight iron hard and make it stop dead, or a seven that will run up the slope. Look at that right side; there's no advantage to the gamble over there.

D: The right side is hardly in play; it has all that rough ground in front, which pushes the ball farther right. The hole must have played differently once, or there would now be no advantage going right. Some pros played the right side during the 1990 Open. Do they ever use the lower edge of this green for a pin position?

T: No.

D: It's too irregular for a cup.

T: This is a new part of the green that's just been built.

D: Much as I admire Walter Woods, this doesn't make sense to me. It's another roller coaster. Extending nature is fine when the ground is reasonable, but surely some of this should have been leveled. I guess we all have our eccentricities.

T: Aye.

The green is relatively open for the second shot.

THE PRINCIPAL'S NOSE

I've always been fascinated by the Principal's Nose Bunker. But I couldn't see the resemblance to a real nose until I drew some sketches of it from every angle in preparation for a hole I was designing in Wakagi, Japan. My client, Seiji Tsutusumi, wanted some features of St. Andrews incorporated in this new course, and the Nose and the Kruger Bunkers seemed ripe for the task. Immediately, I realized, although I doubt I was the first to do so, that it was designed, built, discovered – who knows how it first came into this world – as a hazard for the reverse course. If you walk past Deacon Sime Bunker, which is forty yards from the present front of the Nose, and look backward toward the tee, you can distinguish a magnificent symbol of a nose, a flattened Malay nose maybe, but a powerful example of man-assisted natural sculpture. I find it irresistible. In spite of the proximity to the tee, the Principal's Nose is a great hazard, especially when you have a head wind. Arnie himself has driven a ball into one of the Nose's front bunkers in a qualifying round for the Open, and these are only two hundred yards from the tee. When the Principal's Nose stares you down from the tee, it seems organic, austere, and totally unapologetic for blocking your way. I always think of it as a look-back-in-anger hazard. The Nose I designed for Wakagi, on the other hand, is a more realistic nose, a literal symbol almost twenty feet high with deep flaring nostrils and fifty yards of fairway to the right of it – that's my revenge for driving it over the fence on number sixteen long ago.

17

ROAD

461 YARDS · PAR 4

The famous Road Hole, on which the open has been won several times, but more often lost. The tee is at bottom right and the green at upper left.

T: The best line is over one of the words painted there on the side of that black building. As ye know, it's a reconstruction of the old drying shed on the grounds of the Old Course Hotel. Depending on the wind's direction, we used to play either over the word "Course" or "Hotel." Now, it's over the logo, although "Hotel" would be the spot in a right-to-left wind.

D: Ben Hogan would ask you which letter.

T: He would indeed. In 1984, Tom Watson put his tee shot well right, close to the road, and had a bad moment waiting to learn if he was out of bounds. That was the year he was head-to-head with Ballesteros. Seve, playing in the group in front of Watson, had hit his drive well left, into the rough, then played a great six iron to the green, and made a good four. After learning he was inbounds, Watson took a two iron for his second; it was too much club from where he was, and he hit it across the road near the dike. Tom managed an awkward chip with a seven iron that bounced onto the green and stopped about thirty feet from the cup, but he failed to hole the putt, and took a five. About that time, he heard the roar from eighteen, and knew Ballesteros had birdied. It was a two-shot swing, and Seve had won by two strokes. Alfie Fyles, Watson's caddie, should have been able to stop him from taking that two iron. Many a time I stopped Arnold from playing the wrong club. Ye have to do that, especially when there's pressure on your golfer.

D: What other courses do you caddie on, Tip?

T: I've caddied on every major championship course in Great Britain, but mostly on the Open courses. I caddied for Arnold at the World Match Play at Wentworth. He won the first one, and won again in 1967. I caddied for him when he won the PGA down in Sandwich, shooting 71 in the last round. The wind was blowing about sixty miles per hour, and only four men broke par. He choked down on everything, taking two and sometimes three clubs more than normal. What an exhibition of golf that was! He was a great, *great* player then. Now, I suppose ye'd say he's merely a great player.

D: He's still the most charismatic player in golf, and one of the genuinely nicest people you could hope to meet.

T: I will agree with you about that. For the way he still hits the ball, he should be scoring better than he does. When he was paired with Deane Beman in the Seniors at Turnberry, it was blowing about forty-five miles per hour. Arnold was the favorite. He'd been putting reasonably well, but then he came out for the final round with a brand-new putter, one he'd never used before. I says, "What are ye doing with that?" He says, "Tip, this is a magic wand." Says I, "I don't think ye should do that." Says he, "You don't, eh? Well, this is it." On the sixth green, he made a good putt, maybe twenty yards, for a two. "What did I tell you, Tip?" Says I, "That's good; keep it going." The next hole, his approach is twelve yards from the hole, and he takes *four putts.* I says, "What were ye telling me?" He takes three putts on four more greens and loses the tournament by two shots. If he'd had his usual putter, he'd have won. I'm sure of it.

D: I wonder how often that happens. I thought only Alfie Fyles let his player use the wrong club.

T: That's not fair. Many times I'd tell Arnold: "Ye can't use that club." He'd always say, "Tip, you better be right." On the eleventh hole at Royal Birkdale, he put it in the rough on the right. "Take a seven iron out of the bag," he tells me. "That's too much club," I says. "Okay, Tip, what am I to do?" I told him I'd as soon have an eight iron. "Okay, but you better be right, or I'll be sending you back all the way to St. Andrews," he says. He knocked it six inches from the hole, looked at me, turned to the crowd, and said, "There's only one thing wrong with this game. Tip should be playing, and I should be caddieing."

D: Do you remember any spectacular shots of Arnie's in the Centennial Open?

T: I remember best what happened here on the seventeenth. In the first round, I told him to play a six iron for his approach, and he knocked it in the middle of the green, but took three putts for a five. It was still a par five in those days. The next day, he knocked his tee shot within six feet of where he had been the day before, and put another six iron in the middle of the green; again, he three-putts for a five. On the third day, same drive, knocks it in the middle of the green, and putts for another five. This is where he really lost the Open Championship.

The last day, Arnie's chasing Kel Nagle in one of his famous finishes. He hits almost the same drive, the fourth round in a row he's been just there. He turns to me, and says, "Don't tell me it's a six iron." I says, "Yes, it is." He says, "Give me the five," and I say, "You'll go on the road." "Just watch this," he says. He tried to manufacture the shot, and sure enough, it went on the road. He smiled at me, and said, "Oh, darn." Just to let the crowd know it was no' my fault, he put his arm over my shoulders as we walked down the fairway. Then, with his wedge, he stabs it off the road to within a foot from the pin, and, just like that, gets a four. Walking between the green and the eighteenth tee, Arnold says, "You realize, you've just lost me the Open Championship?" "How's that?" I said. "You've been giving me the wrong club all week," he grinned.

The view from the tee. The professional will aim for the sheds to the left of the hotel and land in the fairway beyond, leaving him a mid-iron to the green.

D: How many men would be that cool or that kind under such pressure?

T: None that I've met. He got a birdie on eighteen, too. So he finished in character. He's been the most exciting golfer since Jones. Nobody could electrify a crowd like Arnold when he was charging at the end of a tournament.

D: Now we need some more of your excellent advice on how to play the hole, Tip.

T: Well, ye can see the Old Course Hotel.

D: How could I miss it?

T: Well, it runs at an angle, so ye have to judge the corner. If there's much wind, there's no' much chance to get home in two.

D: There's a pond in front of the hotel with several balls in it, which you can see from the breakfast room; the hotel is protected by bulletproof glass, which, incidentally, bears the scars and cracks from flying golf balls. You can play to the left, missing the drying sheds altogether, but I cannot imagine anyone coming all this way to St. Andrews without having a go at the famous tee shot over the sheds.

T: That's true. The tee shot's no' as hard as it looks. From the landing area, ye've about two hundred yards left to the green, but ye'd better not go for it. Hit it left.

D: But not too far left, or you're in heavy rough. In 1995, American pro Bill Glasson came to the seventeenth as coleader the second day and hit his first out of bounds. His next went into the deep rough on the left, and he took a nine. In the last round, all the leaders except Mark Brooks found either the road or the Road Bunker.

T: The second is a very demanding shot. Ye must make sure ye're long enough when ye play to the left because if ye're short, ye've the Road Bunker to contend with, and that's bad. Ye're dead when ye're in there.

D: We're all too young to die, especially in the Road Bunker.

T: Myself, I'll play for the front top of the green, but some people are known to go past the trap on the left – sometimes clear up to the eighteenth green – and then come back to the green.

D: Will they chip from the eighteenth tee?

T: Aye; it's a better shot from there because it's flatter.

D: The pin's very far to the left today, a very difficult spot.

T: If the pin's to the extreme left and back, I'd take it away left, with half a club to a club longer, and make sure I got past the trap. Then, as I say, it's

an easy approach – in fact, you could putt it from there. In the days it was played as a par five, all you did was put your second on the right front corner of the green and eight times out of ten, you'd get a four. But, if ye played for a four, ye'd get a six or seven. Ye would'na go wrong playing for a five today.

D: The average player feels himself lucky to get a six.

T: There are very few birdies on this hole, even among the top professionals. Ballesteros and Faldo, the winners here before Daly, played it for a five and each had three fives and a four. Daly got a six and a five the last two rounds, and a four, finally, in the playoff.

D: The crescent slope on the left front of the green pushes the ball away from the hole. If you're anywhere near the bunker, the slope gathers balls and feed them into the bunker. Yet, as I watched this green in 1990 and 1995, I could hardly believe the skill the players demonstrated. They were getting down in two from the road, and sometimes from the bunker as well, in spite of having to hold shots on that glassy surface. A lot of the fellows played their tee shots as far right as possible, followed by a running draw up the length of the green. They were dropping it as near to the front edge as they dared, bouncing the ball toward the hole. A very dangerous shot, that, but those fellows are a breed apart. Most amateurs, and even some professionals, don't have the skill to stop a ball near the hole on this unreceptive

The road, for which the hole is named, runs close by the green and shows the accuracy needed for the second shot if disaster is to be avoided.

green. It would take a Nicklaus in his prime, but even then, there'd be little percentage to the shot even if you were willing to chance a six or a seven.

T: Ballesteros says it's the toughest par four in the world.

D: Yes, and Ben Crenshaw explains why it's the toughest par four – "because it's a par five." Today, the hole is listed at four hundred sixty-one yards, fourteen yards short of a regulation par five. But if the pin's at the far end of the green, the hole's over four hundred eighty yards long. That's a proper par five. As I remember, the road used to have gravel and rough grass along the edges. They used the pitching wedge, then.

T: Aye, the old niblick. Now, it's just tarmac, and the bank is smooth. Nine times out of ten, ye can putt it out.

D: You know, my former partner, Gene Sarazen, invented the sand wedge by putting a thick flange on the niblick. He has poignant memories of St. Andrews.

T: Gene's been in Scotland many times. He's a favorite here. At the Postage Stamp – the eighth at Troon – at the tender age of seventy-one, Gene scored a hole in one in the 1973 Open. Arnold took six at the same hole playing just behind him.

D: That's tournament golf; a five-stroke difference on a single hole. How much of this green is new?

T: Before, the green was *all* on the plateau.

D: The pin for the Open is always behind the Road Bunker. From the wall past the little strip of grass, then across the road, and more grass, the path,

From the fairway, the second shot doesn't look that frightening, except that if you go left you've the impossible Road Bunker and if you go right, you're on the road, with no relief.

another strip of grass, and up the bank, it must be forty to fifty feet to the infamous trap.

T: It's still officially the Road Bunker, but now it's also known as the Sands of Nakajima.

D: Ah, yes, I remember that.

T: Nakajima was in contention in the 1978 Open when he tried a tricky putt along the crown that separates the bunker from the lower part of the green. His ball rolled off the crown and down into the bunker. He was still there in four, and in five, still there in six, out in seven, and took two putts to get down. A nine. He had been playing well up to that point.

D: Poor Tommy. It's one of those incidents that seems to have left a permanent impression on our memories. As a great writer said, There are many of us born with the gift of being able to laugh at misfortunes – of others.

T: He might well have got ten or twelve. I've seen many a ten, and more on his hole, but to get on the green in two, then have a nine, that's rough.

For the Open the pin is always placed about here, behind the bunker. It's possible for a putt to end up in the bunker.

WORKING ON THE MIND

From an architect's point of view, this is a multiple choice hole involving a mildly heroic carry over the drying sheds. The bunkers, the green, and the road are a unique combination of hazards, all working as a troika, just as the Hill and Strath bunkers work in tandem like Scylla and Charybdis, the fabled Rock and Whirlpool of mythology. Each is significant and focal in its own way, not one of them more than the other, but each working tenaciously on your mind. Your thoughts tend to flit from one to another and back again as you weigh your chances for the second shot. The green is long and thin and flat as a calm sea, except for the break in front and the ruffles at the right-hand edge. Originally a par five, as we've mentioned, the green was not designed to hold a long iron shot. Because so many balls are drawn into the bunker after landing on the putting surface, the bunker and the green are locked together.

The bunker itself is deep and wide, with a vertical face of turf bricks. The top of the bunker is much higher than the green, while the sand at the bottom is lower. Hundreds, perhaps thousands, of explosion shots from the depths have built up the lip beside the green, making it progressively more difficult as time passes. It's another example of the handiwork of man, rather than the forces of nature. The road has been the nemesis of so many golfers on an otherwise triumphant round of golf. Like Hell, the Road Bunker and "the road itself" weigh heavily on the mind as you tour the rest of the course. I can think of no other hole in golf that looks so innocent and yet contains so many possibilities for disaster. If you look for symbolic inferences, which I frequently do, the Road Bunker is a man-eater and the placid green is Lorelei luring you into danger; from the golfer's point of view, the Road hole is a monster's monster.

*An interesting view showing the city edging right
up against the eighteenth fairway.*

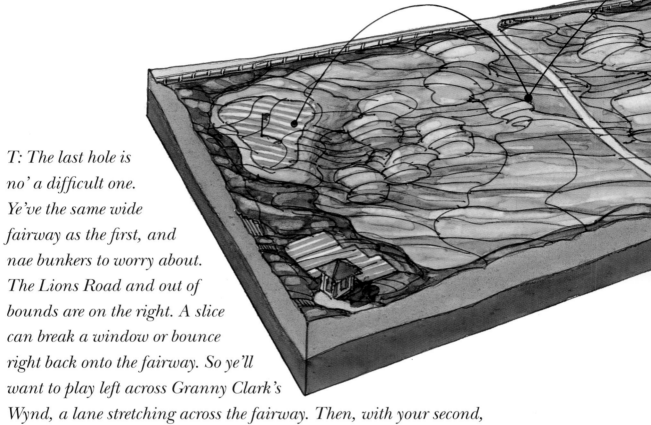

T: The last hole is no' a difficult one. Ye've the same wide fairway as the first, and nae bunkers to worry about. The Lions Road and out of bounds are on the right. A slice can break a window or bounce right back onto the fairway. So ye'll want to play left across Granny Clark's Wynd, a lane stretching across the fairway. Then, with your second, try to avoid the three-foot depression we call the Valley of Sin just before the green. Many good players have come to grief just there.

D: I suspect good players treat a four on seventeen as a birdie and a three on eighteen as a par. It seems fitting, somehow, that the first and eighteenth have a wide open fairway. Where would you aim, Tip?

T: Directly on the monument.

D: Do you mean the tall pillar rising from the grass strip behind the club-house?

T: That's it.

D: They call it the Scotsman lying on his back, but that's a bit of wishful thinking on the part of the Scots.

T: We're a hardy race.

D: Some years ago, I was flying into Prestwick from Boston. When the immigration inspector looked at my passport, he said, "Ah, Muirrrheed, tha's a gude old Scottish name, but a' see ye're from California." I said, "Yes, but you know there are six million Scots in Scotland, and sixty million of Scottish descent in the rest of the world."

"Aye, it's all on account of the kilt," said he.

T: The Germans called us the Ladies from Hell in World War I.

D: I can remember Gene Sarazen telling me he thought the last hole should be a reasonable one, a possible birdie hole, and that the great testing holes should be embedded in the middle of the back nine as they are at Augusta National. I guess that's one point of view. For the opposite, you could cite the very difficult eighteenth holes at Carnoustie and Pebble Beach.

T: Well, both Nicklaus in 1970 and Ballesteros in 1984 birdied this hole when they won here. Doug Sanders three-putted in 1970, missing a three-footer on his second putt. There was a two-stroke swing, and a tie with Nicklaus. Jack won the playoff when he drove to the back of this green, over three hundred sixty yards. Seve has driven the green too.

D: Now they can all drive it with the new clubs they have. But I wonder if you don't have a better chance if you resist the temptation to drive the green and play a carefully controlled second.

T: Most players in the Open will drive to the left toward the monument, as I said. Even if ye drive into the spectators' stands on the left, ye're no' out of bounds and ye'll get a free drop. The right-to-left slope of the green is kinder to the shot coming in from the left side of the fairway.

D: Then there's the Valley of Sin, a hazard that, for sheer simplicity and personality, has few rivals. In the 1990 Open, I noticed Faldo carefully pitching his second well past the pin, chancing a downhill putt just to avoid the Valley of Sin.

T: It's very difficult to judge the speed of putts out of the Valley of Sin. The ball so often fails to climb the slope, or worse still, gets almost to the top, and then rolls back.

D: Yes, it happened to Constantino Rocca in that astonishing climax against Daly in 1995. Who can forget him beating his head on the ground in despair when the ball returned to him, then the stupendous putt through the Valley and across the green into the cup to tie Daly.

T: If ye drive short and right, there are mounds and uneven ground in front of the green that can deflect the ball or give ye a poor lie for your second. Daly drove the green on the third day in 1995, downwind, and nearly went out of bounds. The ball ended up bouncing down the steps of the clubhouse in back of the green. The putt from there was downhill and hard to stop. He got a birdie, but the putt was a character builder. On the last day, he drove way left and pitched onto the green. He almost holed his first putt, but still, it was a much safer strategy at that stage of the tournament.

D: What interests me about this hole is the contrast, a theme that never seems to die on the Old Course. On the one hand, you've this completely flat football field of a fairway with hardly a ripple in it. On the other, the large, steep green that slopes back-to-front and right-to-left with hardly a level putt anywhere. And, of course, the Valley of Sin, which seems to be in

The famous stone bridge over the Burn, with the eighteenth tee to the right out of the photo.

play so often in the finals of important tournaments. The green and the Valley were designed by Old Tom Morris, the great-grandfather and patron saint of golf course architects everywhere.

T: Old Tom left his mark on this Old Course and on this Old Town as no one else has. This hole is named for him.

D: Yes. I've studied his life and that excellent video by David Joy in which he impersonates the Old Man, and now there's a book about him and his golf courses. Old Tom looked after Prestwick and later St. Andrews as resident professional, greenkeeper, clubmaker, and architect, and he designed some great links courses like Royal County Down at Newcastle and Lahinch in Ireland just by walking them with an armful of stakes.

T: That's how they used to do it.

D: I sometimes think the Old Course is the incarnation of Old Tom. His spirit stalks the course like the man from Brigadoon. Soon, a century will have passed and he'll be due here again.

This eighteenth hole has closure. The tall buildings form an outdoor room like those around Central Park in New York, so that when the bleachers are erected on the left for the Open, you have an outdoor theater where the excitement is contained and amplified. This is the true origin of spectator mounds. I find the temporary stands more effective than the permanent spectator mounds on some American courses. The photographers get fine views from the rooftops, as you can see from several examples in this book.

T: Well…what is your final opinion of the Old Course, Desmond, after these last few days?

D: It has all the C's – character, contrast, and choice. There is more character in one hole on this course than in eighteen on the average golf course. Contrast, which is so plentifully evident here, is always a valuable anchor in assessing shots. Choice is the hallmark of twentieth-century life. I think the Old Course is an extraordinary combination of pure nature and the sensitive guidance of man, joining to create a managed landscape in the original spirit of the land. In my opinion, the Old Course is unique – the greatest golf course in the world. And you, Tip?

T: If I felt less than what ye think, Desmond, I would na' be a Scotsman. It's no' so bad, but there's nae better.

The famous clubhouse, the eighteenth green, and the
Valley of Sin, where many a golfer has come to grief.

CLOSING THOUGHTS

As the golfer nears the end of the course, the town returns. By the time he reaches the seventeenth, he's part of the town, albeit the most modern and therefore the ugliest part of it – including an early contemporary building by the late Jim Sterling, Scotland's most famous architect, whose later designs were, fortunately, more human. The second shot and the green at seventeen are assailed by these cold, hard, rectangular piles pleading for a screen of tempering trees and, perhaps, a cloak of Virginia creepers. At the eighteenth, the auld toun opens its arms and embraces golfers as they stroll nearer the green. Town and countryside, buildings and greensward merge as you experience real urban context. You've just played the world's most famous golf course, a rare work of art, and if your heart is in the game, you probably will not be the same again.

APPENDIX

DESMOND MUIRHEAD

When asked about his life, Desmond Muirhead said: "I was due to be born in Scotland but my mother took the wrong train and I was born in Norwich, England. My father never forgave either of us. He was a fanatic golfer with a scratch handicap and he loved the Old Course. He never lived to see me designing golf courses and he would have been so happy to know this is what I do for a living today."

Desmond started his professional career as an urban planner and has recently designed new towns, each housing a hundred thousand people, in Jakarta, Indonesia, and Dubai in the United Arab Emirates. He is also a talented golf course architect with over a hundred courses to his credit in twenty-five countries.

He is best known for the golf courses and surrounding communities of Mission Hills in Palm Springs, California; Muirfield Village in Dublin, Ohio, where the golf course was designed with Jack Nicklaus; Boca West in Florida; and ten golf courses in Japan that have received world attention.

Desmond Muirhead was educated at Bedford School and Cambridge University and many consider that in his recent adventurous work he has raised golf architecture to an intellectual level never before attained.

It is interesting to look at his work on his website at www.golfdesigner.com.

TIP ANDERSON

James Garvie Anderson was first known as "Young Tip" because his father was a caddy who also chalked cues at a local billiards saloon and became known locally as "Tip" Anderson. His son finally outgrew the "Young Tip" moniker and has been known as Tip ever since.

Born in Scotland July 6, 1932, Tip left school at age thirteen, but only took an interest in golf a year later, when he played for the first time. Two years later, at 16, he won the St. Andrews Boys' Championship and went on to win the Fife Boys' Stroke Play Championship at seventeen in 1949. He subsequently became an apprentice clubmaker, but took to caddying in 1957 when the Open Championship was played at St. Andrews. He caddied for Laurie Ayton, a local man, who in fact was joint leader after the first round had been played, but then disappeared into the pack for the rest of the tournament.

Tip's father had been booked by Arnold Palmer's agent when the Centenary of the Open was played at St. Andrews in 1960, but was worried that "there would be too much fuss made of this man," so he gave the bag to his son. In fact, Palmer ended the tournament as runner up to Kel Nagle by one stroke, but won the Open in consecutive years. at Royal Birkdale in 1961 and at Troon in 1962 with Tip.

Today, sitting on his own seat with a plaque above it in the Dunvegan, on the corner of St. Andrews Golf Place, semi-retired Tip reflects on the past forty years. He will tell you that Palmer's chamionship win at Troon in 1962 was probably the best golf Tip has seen, with only one fairway missed in difficult conditions over four rounds. 1964 would be Tip's best year, having won the Open with Tony Lema who, after only one practice round, beat Jack Nicklaus by five shots and declared that the win was 49% himself and 51% Tip Anderson. Palmer, having decided not to come over for the 1964 Open Championship, arrived later in the year for the World Piccadilly Match Play Championship at Wentworth, which he won with Tip.

Today, Tip caddies only occasionally when asked by old clients, such as past British Amateur Champion Joe Carr or his son Roddy, who were part of the winning Walker Cup team at St. Andrews in 1971.

THE 1964 OPEN AT ST. ANDREWS

When Arnold Palmer decided not to come to Scotland for the 1964 Open, Tip was available to caddy for someone else. "Champagne" Tony Lema was one of the outstanding players on the American tour that year, having won four tournaments. His habit of celebrating wins with generous quantities of French champagne endeared him to his fellow golfers and the press, so by the time he appeared at his first British Open he had attained a certain notoriety.

Lema's luck was two-fold: first, Palmer wasn't playing that year after having won two consecutive British Opens in 1961 and 1962 with Tip (he lost in 1960 at St. Andrews by only a stroke when Tip first caddied for him); second, he had secured Tip to guide him around the demanding seaside links, a course with which he was entirely unfamiliar. Lurking in the wings was a young Jack Nicklaus, who had come over for the Open and to whom Lema had lost the Masters by one shot the year before. Lema's first round was a modest but solid 73, but his second round was a 68, a score that set him on his course to victory. Another fine 68 followed, coasting him to a five-stroke win over second-place Jack Nicklaus with a final round of 70 – his first and only major win.

Tragedy struck two years later when Lema's private plane, piloted by himself and with his wife and two other passengers on board, crashed on the 7th hole of the Sportsman's Club golf course in Illinois, killing everyone aboard. He had just played in the PGA Championship and was leaving for an exhibition match in Chicago. One thousand golfers and friends attended his funeral in Los Angeles, including pallbearer Arnold Palmer.

BRITISH OPEN WINNERS
AT ST. ANDREWS

1995 · John Daly, U.S.A. 67, 71, 73, 71

1990 · Nick Faldo, England. 67, 65, 67, 71

1984 · Seve Ballesteros, Spain. 69, 68, 70, 69

1978 · Jack Nicklaus, U.S.A. 71, 72, 69, 69

1970 · Jack Nicklaus, U.S.A. 68, 69, 73, 73

1964 · Tony Lema, U.S.A. 73, 68, 68, 70

1960 · Kel Nagle, Australia. 69, 67, 71, 71

1957 · Bobby Locke, South Africa. 69, 72, 68, 70

1955 · Peter Thomson, Australia. 71, 68, 70, 72

1946 · Sam Snead, U.S.A. 71, 70, 74, 75

1939 · Dick Burton, England. 70, 72, 77, 71

1933 · Denny Shute, U.S.A. 73, 73, 73, 73

1927 · Bobby Jones, U.S.A. 68, 72, 73, 72

1921 · Jock Hutchison, U.S.A. 72, 75, 79, 70

1910 · James Braid, Scotland, 76, 73, 74, 76

1905 · James Braid, Scotland, 81, 78, 78, 81

1900 · J.H. Taylor, England, 79, 77, 78, 75

1895 · J.H. Taylor, England. 86, 78, 80, 78

1891 · Hugh Kirkaldy, Scotland. 83, 83

1888 · Jack Burns, Scotland. 86, 85

1885 · Bob Martin, Scotland. 84, 87

1882 · Bob Ferguson, Scotland. 83, 88

1879 · Jamie Anderson, Scotland. 84, 85

1876 · Bob Martin, Scotland. 86, 90

1873 · Tom Kidd, Scotland. 91, 88

ACKNOWLEDGEMENTS

I have had a lot of help with this book. First, I must thank Tip, without whom it would not have happened at all. Tip's dialogue, which speaks for itself, reveals a man of natural nobility and decency combined with confidence and direct advice. With Tip it is always "we" not "I."

Next I must thank Brian Morgan. The original idea of the book came from Brian, so you could say it would not have happened without him either. He also took the excellent photographs. Indeed he has been called the best photographer of golf courses in the world. He is also a man of great personal charm and a dear friend of many years.

Another friend, John Strawn, – a first-rate writer in his own right with a seminal book, *Driving the Green,* to his credit – did research for me, including several visits to St. Andrews, helping mightily with the introduction.

Alan Beveridge, of the St. Andrews Trust who was a general inspector, was his usual courteous self, ready with advice and information.

David Joy, of Old Tom Morris fame, generously gave me a paragraph from his forthcoming biography of Tip.

Cal Brown, another excellent writer, gave the entire book the scouting of his expert eye and served as the official editor. Cal has many books on golf to his credit and is a former Editor of the formidable *Golf Digest* magazine.

My friend David Smith did an outstanding job on the graphic representation of the golf holes – even to redrawing some where I thought the line of flight was misleading.

St. Andrews' great former superintendent, Walter Woods, was unfailingly courteous and generous with his time and information.

My old friend Bob Reid, who to my mind is still up there with the best book designers in the world, designed the book not once, but three times, and supervised production of it through his New York connections in the book trade.

Lastly, my secretary Ella, who types a hundred words a minute and can take shorthand as fast as I can talk, typed the manuscript at least three times.

I am sure I've left some deserving people out of these acknowledgements. Please contact me, if so, and I will see that they are included in any other editions.

I enjoyed writing it, and hope everyone who reads this book will get the reflection of both Tip's and my enthusiasm for this whole project.

— DESMOND MUIRHEAD